Creative Business

Also by Chris Genasi:

*Corporate Community Investment: How to Make Your Business
     Profitably Popular*
Winning Reputations: How to be Your Own Spin Doctor

Acknowledgements

The various quotes in this book have been taken from the website
www.creativityforlife.com. Their assistance is much appreciated.

Every effort has been made to trace all the copyright holders but if
any have been inadvertently overlooked the publishers will be
pleased to make the necessary arrangements at the first opportunity.

CREATIVE BUSINESS

ACHIEVING YOUR GOALS THROUGH CREATIVE THINKING AND ACTION

Tim Bills

and

Chris Genasi

palgrave
macmillan

To Jill, Grace and Louis, and to my parents. (C. G.)

To Alicia, Sam, Emily, Mom and Dad;
and to Chris for inviting me along for the ride. (T. B.)

First published 2003 by
PALGRAVE MACMILLAN
Houndmills, Basingstoke, Hampshire RG21 6XS and
175 Fifth Avenue, New York, N.Y. 10010
Companies and representatives throughout the world

PALGRAVE MACMILLAN is the global academic imprint of the Palgrave Macmillan division of St. Martin's Press, LLC and of Palgrave Macmillan Ltd. Macmillan® is a registered trademark in the United States, United Kingdom and other countries. Palgrave is a registered trademark in the European Union and other countries.

ISBN 0–333–99735–2 paperback

This book is printed on paper suitable for recycling and made from fully managed and sustained forest sources.

A catalogue record for this book is available from the British Library.

Library of Congress Cataloging-in-Publication Data

Bills, Tim, 1961–
    Creative business: achieving your goals through creative thinking and action / Tim Bills and Chris Genasi.
        p. cm.
    Includes bibliographical references and index.
    ISBN 0–333–99735–2 (pbk.)
    1. Creative ability in business. I. Genasi, Chris. II. Title.

    HD53.B55 2003
    658.4′063--dc21

                                                                        2003056340

Editing and origination by
Curran Publishing Services, Norwich

10 9 8 7 6 5 4 3 2 1
12 11 10 09 08 07 06 05 04 03

Printed and bound in Great Britain by
Creative Print & Design (Wales), Ebbw Vale

CONTENTS

LIST OF FIGURES AND TABLES

Figures

Table

CHAPTER 1

How creativity can change your world – again

Introduction: what is creativity?

'There is no greater joy than that of feeling oneself a creator. The triumph of life is expressed by creation.'

HENRI BERGSON

It's a slippery concept, creativity: every time you get close to coming to grips with it, it seems to slip away, as indefinable as ever. Although all of us are familiar with terms such as brainstorming, lateral thinking and innovation, which are commonly used in the commercial world, the notion of creativity with its many artistic connotations has only recently become more widely used in business circles. However, as business grows ever more complex, we believe that this trend of wider usage and appreciation is set to gather pace as creative thinking becomes increasingly recognised as the essential process by which the most innovative ideas are formed and the toughest problems are solved.

So what precisely is creativity? As anyone who has delved into the question of what exactly constitutes it will know, the notion of creativity means something very different from one individual to another. It is for this reason that we offer our own definition from the outset as follows:

The capacity to challenge the existing order of things, by deliberately forcing ourselves out of our usual way of thinking, to see the status quo from a new and enlightening perspective, to form new ideas and find practical ways to implement change in the light of fresh insights.

The fact that we will be focusing specifically on creativity in business has certainly helped us to formulate a reasonably precise definition. Our belief is that with practice, and the regular application of the techniques detailed later on in the book, there will be much less need for you to force yourself to think creatively: it will simply become a part of the natural course of each working day.

As you will see later in this chapter, one of our first goals is to help you see clearly that we all possess an innate capability to be creative. To do that, we hope to de-mystify the concept of creativity and point out that, like many skills, creativity can be improved through practice, that even the most gifted amongst us often need to collaborate and that they almost always seek inspiration from the work and invention of others.

In Chapters 2 and 3, we will look at the enemies of creativity: at how once-thriving creative powers and vision can so easily become suffocated, even to the point of being choked to death. We will show you how to combat these adversaries and how you can start to re-connect with your creative potential once again. In later chapters, we will take you through a range of flexible tools that will help you to re-calibrate your focus in the light of a newly galvanised vision of the future. These techniques will help you to discover your real goals by looking at them from radically new perspectives and help you overcome the hurdles that prevent you from fulfilling those ambitions. By doing this, we will show that the path required may well be a very different one from the one that you are presently pursuing; that the obstacles currently being negotiated are in fact illusory; and that once the real barriers are identified, they can often be easily resolved. The creative process can then start again, only the next time, it will be focused on a much more clearly defined set of objectives and goals.

And while this book is essentially designed to help you solve problems in your business, we have also addressed the issue of creativity from a personal viewpoint and, where appropriate, placed it in that context. We feel that in many ways individuals are facing exactly the same issues in their private lives that businesses are in the commercial world, and since we believe that the two perspectives are inextricably linked, the personal angle cannot, and should not, be ignored.

So we make no apology for making the connection between the two: if we can learn to improve our personal lives through more creative thinking then we can do the same for our businesses, and vice versa.

First, though, we want to start by exploring in more detail why creative thinking matters so much, how re-acquainting yourself with it can improve many aspects of your life, and to consider exactly why creativity in business is so important in today's world.

Creativity matters

'Some men throw their gifts away on a life of mediocrity, great men throw everything they have into their gifts and achieve a life of success.'

GREG WERNER

Competition, the constant ebb and flow of the global economy and the inevitability of major, unforeseen events mean that we are always going to be faced with awkward situations, threats and difficult challenges as well as exciting new opportunities, usually arriving abruptly with very little advanced warning. Helping you to learn how to resolve problems, how to better place yourself to take the chances that life throws at us and exploit those opportunities is what this book is all about.

Creative minds shape the world we live in. We all take enormous pleasure in the creativity evident in the music we listen to, the paintings we admire and the architectural feats we marvel at. And almost everything we do or touch on a daily basis in the work place or at home involves an object or concept that has been invented by someone, somewhere. Creativity is all around us and it continues to change our world, and at a quickening pace. It is a force that impacts upon every aspect of our businesses, careers and personal lives, and yet for most of us, creative thinking is what a very small number of other people do; being creative is somebody else's job.

Yet if we are to enjoy the rewarding lives that we have always striven for, then we are going to have to take more control of them. Today, our lives are in serious danger of becoming submerged under the burden of expectation as we try to meet increasingly improbable deadlines, chase after each new technological advancement and navigate our way through a deluge of red tape and detail. Many of us recognise that there is a problem; we may even know what is causing it, and almost certainly we will be trying to resolve it. But as each day goes by, the complexity of life only seems to increase yet further, and our ability to break out of the cycle weakens under its weight.

If we're to keep our heads above water, we need to find a way to get away from this whirlpool to calmer waters and – even if only for a brief moment – to rise above all the time-consuming responsibilities we have, and look at the world with clearer vision and greater clarity of thought. We need to think smarter – much smarter. To do that, we need to think creatively and, as we stated in our definition, begin the process of forcing ourselves out of our usual way of thinking, to see things from new and enlightening perspectives, to form new ideas and find practical ways to implement change in the light of fresh insights.

Initially, breaking the cycle will probably require us to take some small steps before we can fully begin the process of regeneration, of bringing back some order and thinking space into our lives. You don't have to be in the running for a Nobel Prize to be capable of using creative thinking to make a big difference. In fact, the better practised you become on the smaller problems, the better equipped you will be to deal with the bigger challenges that will inevitably come along. Creative thinking already lies at the heart of many successful and progressive businesses, and since it forms part of their daily thinking, all problems and opportunities are essentially approached in the same way, regardless of size. And as creative as those businesses are recognised as being, they all had to start somewhere.

One of our key starting points will be to recognise the symptoms of creative decay, to identify the causes and be aware of the damage that results. If we can do that, we have made our first significant step away from the creativity crisis, and with a sound appreciation of why creative thinking matters we can then work towards a new way of thinking that will reap significant rewards. In short, we can start to see how much creative thinking can change our businesses, lives and careers. Despite the many obstacles that lie in the way, the value that is placed on creative expression has never been greater, but it hasn't always been that way . . .

Creativity's hip

'There are no problems – only opportunities to be creative.'
DORYE ROETTGER

For much of history, thinking creatively has been the preserve of an extremely small number of people. The vast majority of the world's population carried out the instructions of those few individuals and their leaders. Whether it was building the pyramids or fighting a battle, most people simply followed orders and concentrated on survival in a difficult and often very hostile environment. The scope for creative thinking for the average person was pretty much non-existent: in some periods of history it barely reared its head at all. Indeed, for many centuries the consequence of expressing anything 'out of the box' was at best to be ridiculed or at worst an untimely death.

However, as time has passed, social conditions have increasingly become more conducive to, and tolerant of, creative thought and freedom of expression. Perhaps the 1960s illustrated this process most vividly, and in more recent decades the dramatic increases in technological development, availability of information, wealth and opportunity, have allowed many more of us to tap into our own innate creativity.

Through the Internet, we can freely source information on any subject from all over the world and absorb other cultures and experiences into our own way of thinking. And for many, e-mail, although a threat to verbal communication, has rekindled the largely forgotten art of letter writing. Digital photography has eradicated those disappointing trips to the local developer and replaced them with the freedom to be experimental – we no longer have to factor in the cost of dozens of shots that were thought 'interesting' at the time – and those vastly more creative images can then be manipulated in an infinite number of ways. All of this, and more, gives freer rein to our creative juices.

In the corporate world, not only do businesses and the people they employ now have more tools at their disposal, they have the stimulus of growing competition, not only in straightforward commercial terms but also in terms of the creative process itself. There is only one way to keep up with, or surpass, a competitor who has just produced the best value product in the marketplace, launched the most compelling advertising campaign seen in years or revolutionised their customer service levels – and that is to be equally or even more creative.

Gradually, more and more businesses are placing greater weight on the value and contribution of creativity and innovation; they are starting to factor this into their recruitment selection criteria and are now providing a culture that is more conducive to, and rewarding of, innovative thinking. The reason that this is happening in so many more businesses is not simply because they are choosing to do it; it is because they are finding that they have to.

But whatever the motive for embracing it is, the ability to think creatively in an increasingly instinctive manner and successfully harness the innovation it produces is now, more than ever, a defining characteristic of today's most forward thinking and successful businesses.

Creativity is universal

If creative thinking is to become a habit, we need to know how to go about unlocking the creative potential that we all have. To do this, we first have to accept that creativity is not the sole preserve of entrepreneurs, inventors and those working in the arts. In this respect, we make three key observations:

- You don't have to be a genius to be creative. Innate creativity varies from one individual to another, but being creative is a learning process and, like any other skill, will improve with practice. Hard work counts for something.

- Even the gifted collaborate. Our creativity may at worst be simply dormant. Creativity is often stimulated most noticeably through interaction, often through collaboration with the right person or mix of people.

■ All creative people are heavily influenced by, and seek inspiration from, others' work and performance.

You don't have to be a genius to be creative

'If you can't excel with talent, then triumph with effort.'

DAVE WEINBAUM

Of course it helps, but you truly do not have to be a genius to be creative, the fact is that we all have creative potential; whether we use it or not is another issue. Our first step towards a more creative and enterprising existence must be to accept our own innate creativity.

Yet, how many of us would instinctively agree that this innateness really exists? Of course, those who work in creative fields readily appreciate the universality of creativity but the rest of us, the majority, tend to see it as the preserve of the gifted few. Maybe it is a question of modesty or human nature but however much more skilful, experienced and inventive we become, we still seem quicker to recognise genuine creativity in others rather than ourselves.

We usually associate creativity with extremely gifted people, who obviously form a very elite group. They are often characterised as unconventional, anti-establishment types who are rather eccentric and in some cases are more than just a few sandwiches short in their picnic box. Many people also see creative types as being unaware of, and thoroughly disconnected from, the real world.

Genius is a highly subjective concept and is unfortunately too easily attributed to the wrong people; real genius lies at the extreme edge of the creative spectrum and is unquantifiable. In reality, many of those that might be regarded as being touched by the hand of genius are equally known for the extraordinary hours and energy that they put into their work, much of which results in 'failed' experiments or blind alleys. They find their answers through a meticulous and painstaking process of elimination, the solution ultimately revealing itself under the sheer weight of numbers or even yielding to that most fickle of masters, luck: that essential but ephemeral ingredient that can solve everything in a single moment.

What really singles these people out is often nothing more than sheer hard work focused upon a very narrow field: a dogged persistence allied to creative powers that intrinsically, are not so much greater than our own. Of course this may be a wild oversimplification, but it is vitally important that we begin to see the gifted amongst us as a little less superhuman and a little more of this earth. Exceptional as many of these individuals undoubtedly are, they face many of the same obstacles and frustrations that we do.

As we have said, the difficulty many of us have in embracing our creative selves is exacerbated by the fact that we tend to associate creativity with a variety of professions that represent a very small percentage of the population: entrepreneurs, inventors, artists, sculptors, writers, cartoonists, poets, composers and so on. And in making a particular association with genius, we may fail to recognise that creativity, like all skills, varies enormously in its degree and to a great extent, has to be learnt – and once learnt, practised. Not possessing a creative mind to the same degree as those renowned for their creativity does not mean that we don't have one at all or that hard work cannot make up much of the difference.

If the majority of us feel that creativity is something that only a few fortunate souls are blessed with and so essentially deny its potential within ourselves, how are we to improve our problem solving ability, deal more effectively with our horribly complicated lives, advance our careers and fulfil our potential?

The fact is that although true genius (whatever that is) may lie beyond us, we are all nevertheless capable of moments of genius. Indeed, we may have already produced several such moments but failed to find the commitment or support to develop them. Often, when we discover a novel idea, we assume someone else has already discovered it. Imagine the inital excitement that an amateur guitarist might experience when happening across a new chord sequence or that a cook might relish in when imagining a new utensil that would make light of some culinary battle they are engaged in. The ecstacy almost always gives way to resignation: that it must have been used before in the case of our guitarist, or that our chef's new gadget has surely already been patented.

Over the centuries, how many novel ideas or inventions have occurred to hundreds, or even thousands, of ordinary individuals? And yet, only one can be credited with having made the discovery. In truth, the question of who or what deserves the credit is not a straightforward one, but answering it can throw a good deal of light on the type of culture our businesses should aspire to. A discovery can be the result of teamwork, or of a positive business approach to environment, innovation and risk, or of a government that is supportive to new ideas through funding programs and the minimising of red tape.

Creativity is not simply a means for an elite minority to produce an artistic or technological work of the highest order; it is a tool that allows all of us to look at the world differently, facilitating our view through the thickening fog to increasingly frequent moments of clarity, and as a result achieve development and growth on all levels and in all aspects of our lives. The aim for businesses is to harness that potential by providing the environment, culture and ethos in which idea creation is fostered, acted upon and rewarded. The first stage is to accept that our own creative potential is waiting for us to tap into it – and we don't have to be geniuses.

Even the gifted collaborate: one plus one can make three

While the potential for creative thinking exists in us all, most of us need something or someone to help bring it to the surface. The creative spark we need is often the product of two or more minds interacting in a manner that probes, questions and challenges the preconceived notions of each collaborator.

In the theatre or film world, this is what is often referred to as 'chemistry', whereby two elements interact and become more highly charged, their creative powers more pronounced. A third, indefinable charge comes to life somewhere between the two protagonists. It is when one plus one actually can make three. The result of this sort of chemistry is not simply a much more refined performance from each individual, it also produces something entirely new, something that can lie at the real heart of innovation. The list of famous collaborators is virtually endless. If we think of examples such as Lennon and

McCartney or Gilbert and Sullivan, we think no less of their individual creative abilities because they were 'only' one part of a partnership. And the partners do not need to be equal in energy or creative ability. The success of a creative partnership relies much more on its unique chemistry than on the partners bringing equal 'talent' to the table.

The analogy of the chemistry between actors can be used to consider your own circumstances. Who do you interact with? Are they the right people or do you need to find a better blend of skills and personalities to provide a genuine spark? And the teams that are employed in your business: are they working to their full potential? Do conflict or conservatism reign where collaboration and creativity should prosper? Are your teams becoming stale? Do you need to start mixing them up a little?

In business, creativity is rarely the product of a single individual, although when it is those gifted individuals usually attract most of the headlines, giving the impression that this is the way creativity usually works. In fact, great ideas are usually the result of one or more teams of creative people working in an environment and culture that encourages and fosters innovative thinking. And like a family home that strives for harmony and enrichment, the people responsible for those teams need to be tolerant of 'mistakes' but also pragmatic in their pursuit of their own definitions of success.

The adage that a problem shared is a problem halved largely reflects the way that the process of interaction can shed light on and clarify the issue in question and show the way forward. Often, the simple act of verbally disclosing a problem brings out much of the solution long before any dialogue has started.

Yet how many of us have difficulty in recognising the importance of interaction, of sharing ideas and problems? For too many, seeking help is felt to be a sign of weakness, even of failure. We lack faith in the innate benevolence of human nature: most people are more than happy to respond positively to a genuine call for help. If anything, they regard the ability to ask for assistance when necessary as a positive attribute, indeed as a strength, recognising that so few of us engage others in solving our problems anything like as often as we should.

Take first generation owner-managers for example. For those who have single-handedly built up their own businesses, discussing problems in an open and inviting manner can be a difficult skill to acquire since it was their initiative and drive alone that was largely responsible for the initial success. They get used to making commercial decisions (good or bad) very much on their own, and when their overall strategy has led to success, closed decision making can be a very difficult habit to break.

However, as a business grows and more key people are required to manage and drive it forward, there is an increasing need for a more open style of management and for strategy to become much more of a collaborative process. If real expansion is to be achieved, then delegating responsibility to a capable and creative team of people is absolutely fundamental.

As we shall see later in the book, whether we are talking about a privately owned business or a huge international conglomerate, character traits such as perfectionism and fear are considerable blockers to collaboration and delegation, and are found in all parts of the business and at all levels.

In a growing business, the re-apportionment of responsibility never stops and that philosophy has to be passed down through, and along, all tiers of management. As a company expands, those in senior roles need to temper their own natural inclinations to act unilaterally. This is not to say that they should compromise their ability to make decisions – that remains a defining characteristic of the entrepreneur – but that they should increasingly seek to attract the best talent and having done so, listen to it, embrace the notion of teamwork and trust it. As a business becomes more complex, so does the chemistry. The challenge for senior management is to maintain at all times the conditions that foster the sparks of inventiveness that every business needs to thrive.

Size isn't everything: influence and inspiration

'The creative person wants to be a know-it-all. He wants to know about ancient history, nineteenth-century mathematics, manufacturing techniques, flower arranging, and hog futures. Because he never knows when these ideas might come together to form a new idea.'

CARL ALLY

Erroneously, we often think that highly creative people possess a deep well of innate creativity that is largely untouched by external influences: all they have to do is tap into it whenever they choose and off they go.

It is certainly true that some people have greater natural reserves of inventiveness than others, but creative expression is more about merging the creative talent you have with a sponge-like ability to absorb influences from a variety of sources and thereby create another, entirely new take on the world. Of course some people's pores are larger than others', but like many things in life – size isn't everything – it is all about using what you have. If we use our sponges daily, keep them free of mildew and at their most porous, our creative output may ultimately exceed that of many of the more gifted among us.

In this sense too, just as with direct collaboration whose importance we have already considered, creativity is far from a solitary activity: our interaction with the world around us and its influences is every bit as real as with a collaborator sitting at the opposite end of the room.

Without consciously looking, creative individuals are constantly receptive to new ideas from outside their normal field of expertise, regularly seeing parallels between all sorts of seemingly unassociated daily occurrences and their chosen professions: TV adverts, the way plant life regenerates, something a child says. Such people don't have to force themselves to do this, it just happens naturally: a part of their brain is always quietly on the lookout, which is why novel ideas are so often produced during moments of relaxation when that part of the brain is unhindered. This book will teach you to be more like them by helping you to form a habit of drawing inspiration from the world around you.

Businesses, too, need to be more receptive to outside influences; there is a great deal that can be learnt from how other companies innovate, regardless of which sector or geographical region they operate in. Time needs to be found on a regular basis to stand back from the fire fighting and look at our businesses in a much broader context, to see how others behave and apply the lessons we learn to our own businesses.

It is not cheating to be influenced by others: it shows that we can recognise originality when we see it, and the mere act of acknowledging it and soaking it up serves to exercise our own creative muscle, making it more responsive and powerful. Without exception, anybody that has inspired us has been inspired by something or someone else; it has always been that way. Oasis are influenced by The Beatles who in turn were inspired by black R & B, Bo Diddley, Chuck Berry, Carl Perkins and so on; and before long there will be a whole new generation of artists citing Oasis as their major influence. In business, management's role is to provide that inspiration and demonstrate an outward-looking commitment to new ideas and innovation by providing the right environment for imaginative thinking and interaction among people working in different departments and even different companies.

There are a number of creative techniques that you will see later in the book that will ask you to seek inspiration from others including:

- *Copycat.* In which you will be asked to imagine something that you like or admire – a company, celebrity, politician, a public figure or an institution – and list these attributes and behaviours and then think how you could apply these to your own business or specific problem.

- *Disney takeover.* You will imagine that the Disney Corporation will be taking over your business tomorrow and consider what changes this highly successful firm will make to every aspect of your business. By simply borrowing the Disney mindset for half an hour, you should be able to stretch your latent imaginative powers and identify many changes that could be made right now with your existing management team.

- *Turncoat.* You will be asked what you would do if you started to work for your most admired competitor; your goal is to exploit everything you know to damage your current business. From this point of view, you will see a vast number of new insights into your firm's weaknesses and its strengths. You will be able to take an unsentimental view of your business and as a result protect it from threats.

You will be empowered by these thought processes as new light is cast over every aspect of your business.

Inspiration from the creativity of others and the world around us should be purposely sought after, acknowledged and embraced. There are millions of ideas out there, scattered across every walk of life; all we need to do is get better at spotting them, building on them and linking them to our own field of expertise. Identifying a creative idea, linking it and applying it is a theme that we will return to again and again.

We have now looked at the nature of creativity, why it is so important and why we should not feel afraid to accept that everyone has creative power. To throw more light on where those powers are, or have disappeared to, we now need to look at the enemies of the creative process: at how and why our creativity goes into hibernation.

CHAPTER 2

Why creativity goes into hibernation

Time management and the creativity crisis

'Learn to pause . . . or nothing worthwhile will catch up to you.'

DOUG KING, POET

Paradoxically, many of the technological advances and innovations that allow a greater expression of our creative abilities are also working strongly against us. On a business level, shortening product cycles and increased global competition are competing with increasing red tape to rob us of the time in which we need to think.

On a personal level, the pace and complexity of modern life has also become a serious inhibiter to creative thinking since it so often destroys the climate we need to be able to solve problems or visualise an alternative future. We know that something is fundamentally wrong, we feel strongly that things could be so much better, but all too often we simply lack the time and space to even contemplate change, let alone evaluate, identify and implement it. The pace of change is running ahead of our ability to adapt to it and the gaps between those chasing it are getting wider. This is undoubtedly good news for those that are leading the pack but the rest are in danger of falling so far behind that they will never catch up.

Information overload, which is coinciding with a growing awareness of the importance of creative thinking, re-evaluation and innovation, is resulting in something of a mania for change. We are all being encouraged to be more creative and embrace change, but many of us are clueless about how to move forward. And the number suffering from this predicament is growing.

The result is that too many individuals and businesses are falling out of the race altogether. They are left staring at change as a rabbit does at oncoming headlights in the dark – and we all know what happens to rabbits: they either get out of the way or they get run over.

Either way, they are left behind and in the commercial world that means going out of business, and probably sooner rather than later.

If businesses are to succeed then they need to be the ones with the headlights, dipping them to see the day-to-day operational issues and the seeds of tomorrow's great ideas, but regularly using full beam to see clearly the signs and mileposts that tell us that we are still heading in the right direction. Adjusting their spread from time to time will also be necessary, throwing light on each flank so that any opportunities for a rewarding detour can be taken and any threats to off-road us avoided.

The need to think creatively is thus more acute than ever, not least in the sense that we need to be much more inventive in the way we manage the increased complexity of our lives and our businesses. Later on in the book we will look at a range of quick and easy to use techniques specifically designed to help you break out of the catch-22 of not having enough time to think.

In business, the need to re-invent ourselves, or undergo some form of major re-structuring, occurs with a frequency that has dramatically increased in recent years. But all too often, re-structuring is only embarked upon as a response to some sort of crisis. It is forced upon us and the motive is survival rather than advances; too many businesses treat change like the 'whining schoolboy' in Shakespeare's *As You Like It*, who was found 'creeping like snail/Unwillingly to school'.

By contrast, regular re-invention, as part of a deep understanding and acceptance of change, is the accepted norm for progressive businesses that want to do much better than simply survive.

In large part this phenomena has been driven by innovation and technological advance, which is having a profound affect on every function of our businesses. To compete, we need more efficient and more powerful software, leaner administration, more efficient methods of production and distribution, more intelligent marketing. And as we all know, technological advance has a habit of feeding on itself in an exponential way.

There is exponential growth too, in the various forms of communication we all have to deal with – e-mails, portable phones, pagers, blackberries, bleeping PDAs and text messages – all of which keep us informed but also rob us of crucial thinking time. In a way, these too have a habit of feeding on themselves: we now find ourselves having to look into e-mail management systems, define procedures to prevent internet abuse, create policies and procedures for the use of mobile phones and laptops – the list goes on and on.

Globalisation and the dramatic changes in the major economies of the world have resulted in many more of us having to commute to work: another significant drain on our time. Sitting in a plane, train or automobile is no substitute for face-to-face contact and interaction. And if we were able to use all those lonely hours of commuting to enrich our lives with audio cassettes and the like, we would all be able to speak four languages by now with a masters degree in the subject of our choice as a bonus. But we cannot: almost every hour spent in a car is a wasted one, public transport is tedious and unreliable, and air travel is often cramped and invariably exhausting.

It is a wonder how any of us can cope with it all. And at a time when strategic thinking has become a daily necessity, businesses are having to deal with a massive increase in rather more mundane issues: more red tape to negotiate and more form filling on behalf of the tax office, the implementation of 'quality control' procedures that have little to do with the actual quality of our products and services, environmental issues and community relations, human resources management and the need to deal with an ever more litigious society.

And since the major financial scandals that have arisen as a result of the one type of creativity we won't be recommending – creative accounting – all businesses are now being required to be yet more transparent, which means even more red tape.

It is not as if many of us get much respite at home any more. There are so many more distractions – computer games, a greater range of leisure activities, hobbies, different ways of seeking entertainment, more restaurants, more films, more disposable income – simply more of everything.

While many of these things can and do enhance our lives, having too much of them has the same effect as going to work and finding that we have 63 messages in our inbox after just a single day off. They deprive us of those crucial spaces in our lives that are required for creative thought, for regeneration, for seeing the bigger picture.

And if this is true of the average family, where does it leave the growing number of parents that are either separated or divorced? For them, the serious disruption caused by the separation is gradually replaced by a way of life that is stretched to the extreme through the need to dash between one family home and the other, travelling greater distances and juggling more and more.

Thus, just when we need to find more time to stand back and think, most of us find that there is more and more in our working and daily lives that prevents us from doing so. As time goes by it seems that we are required to resolve the enormous range of problems that modern life relentlessly throws at us in less and less time, and therein lies the vicious circle in which many of us find ourselves. If more and more of us are finding ourselves fighting on far too many fronts, we are not going to just lose some battles: we are in danger of losing the war.

And if we are this stretched by the daily grind, how will we cope with the major upheavals that inevitably visit our lives – often unexpectedly – such as a sudden buy-out opportunity, a change of occupation or role, moving house, parenthood or even a combination thereof? We need more capacity, and at the moment we have very little. It is therefore not surprising that, for most of us, our creative potential is never fully realised.

And yet it is frequently these upheavals that bring out the innate creativity that usually lies so dormant. In other words, our ability to think in a new and novel way is often only awakened when we find we are getting backed into a corner or find ourselves under extreme pressure. But if we only think creatively when it is forced upon us, when a problem or a series of problems becomes so grave that we are finally forced to think seriously about a given situation and take action, what damage may have been wreaked in the meantime?

If only we could find time to stand back from the detail, the minutiae of modern life, and think more creatively, perhaps the many problems we face could be identified so much earlier and, being smaller, be more easily resolved. If creative thinking is only ever going to be a knee-jerk response to a crisis, some of us are going to be in for a lot more trouble than we can imagine.

Occasionally, we are going to get away with it: we will pull ourselves back from the brink of bankruptcy or save our marriage before our differences become irreconcilable. But if creative thinking has never been a part of our lives, or has recently ceased to be, then the chances are we're going to get caught out before long and it will almost certainly be too late to rescue ourselves from the crisis.

We do not want that to happen. Our aim is for this book to help you to find time to think in a creative way as part of your daily life; to identify problems and solve them along the way so that when a major problem does come along, as it surely will, you will recognise the signs early and be better equipped to prevent it from becoming a catastrophe.

In Chapter 6 there are two creative techniques that specifically address the issue of time as a constraint on your creative powers:

- *The oldest worker in town* (page 104). Whereby you imagine that you have another 100 years before retirement, that time is no longer a problem for you. How would you now approach the business? What sort of hours would you work? How would your priorities change? What type of things would you still treat as a priority despite the longer time horizon?

- *Sleepless in battle* (page 105). Imagine you did not need to sleep and there were suddenly 48 hours in every day. What sort of things would you do with your extra time? What things would still be a nuisance and how might you deal with them now you had more time? The discussion is designed to identify some key priorities and we hope will stimulate ideas for ensuring these are built into the real working day, as well as highlighting those elements that should be reduced or avoided.

Are you passionate?

'Success is not the key to happiness. Happiness is the key to success. If you love what you are doing, you will be successful.'

ALBERT SCHWEITZER

Creativity isn't just about solving problems; it's about finding a way to get back in touch with yourself and your business, and re-directing both in a way that matches them much more closely with your real goals. For too many of us, the burning ambition that we once had – or perhaps any kind of ambition – has been replaced by resignation, complacency, caution and conservatism. We need to turn that around, and we need to set new goals in the short, medium and long term.

In essence, we need to know a great deal more about where we are heading so that we can recalibrate our path accordingly and ensure that our decision making is now made in that context. We must do so in the sure knowledge that nothing stays the same. Our personal lives, careers and businesses will often lose focus, at times they will wander from the path we have set ourselves and they will occasionally be prone to being blown completely off course by as yet unforeseen events; they will always need calibration. And why should we ever expect it to be otherwise? It is a fact of life that our aims and ambitions will need to be constantly modified in the light of experience and an ever-changing world.

It is not just books of this genre that can show how easily our lives and careers can go wrong and, conversely, how easy it can be to start turning them around. For example, how many books and articles have been written on the subject of how to revitalise our sex lives and relationships? Thousands, and all of them ask us to recollect those things that attracted us to our partners in the first place, to consider the many creative ways in which we pursued the relationship in its early stages, and to think again in the present of how we can inject some of the spirit and enterprise that once came so instinctively.

If we were to find a single word that sums up the emotion and drive that made the initial progress of our relationships such a rewarding and productive experience, it would be passion.

The analogy is clear. Our embers may burn low from time to time but if we choose careers and businesses for which we are passionate, then thinking in an imaginative way is not something that we do out of duty or as a response to reading this book, but something that we do naturally. Our subconscious effortlessly works away on problems, large or small, to find solutions and the whole process feels less like work and a lot more like play: our energy and commitment are given unconditionally.

On a more practical level, those books and articles do not place much value on grand gestures: it is usually too late for those. They tend to concentrate on the many small things that can and do make a real difference when they are employed on a regular basis. Businesses are no different; attention to the simple things is required on an on-going basis in order to keep the bigger picture in focus and the embers of creativity glowing.

In the following sections, we will be looking at the ways in which enthusiasm and passion go into hibernation, sometimes to the point of being frozen under a permafrost. Before we do that, ask yourself the question: are *you* passionate?

Creative techniques that can help you to assess how passionate you are in relation to your business or profession include:

- *Kids' stuff* (page 101). Imagine you had to explain your business problem to a group of 10-year-olds; how would you do it? How would you make your business appealing, what sort of events would you hold to promote your firm? Think about the type of people you could enlist to help you reach this group. By thinking about your business and its problems from this perspective you will be forced to simplify issues and consider the fundamentals involved from the ground up. The ease with which you can do this will tell you much about how deeply you understand the business you are in.

- *Teenage kicks* (page 102). In which you are required to imagine that you had to promote your business to teenagers: how would you capture their imagination? How would you make your firm appear trendy and stylish? What techniques taken from teen culture might you use to bring your business to life? Try to see the world through their eyes and think what would impress them. Later you can see which aspects appeal to you and consider how they might be applied to your actual business problems.

- *Ovation* (page 106). Imagine you are receiving a standing ovation: what would you need to have done to have earned it? This technique is all about envisioning success by imagining the things you would need to have accomplished to deserve such acclaim from your peers. Standing ovations are almost entirely reserved for those who are have a strong passion for what they do, and this technique forces you to reflect on your current position and work out the gaps between where you are now and where you need to be if you are to receive an ovation.

- *Starting over* (page 115). Imagine you were starting in your business again: what would you do differently and what would you still do in the same way? If you were facing the same issues at the same time as starting again, would you approach them in different ways? Would you choose another line of work? This exercise allows you to mentally throw away all the baggage you have accumulated over the years and look at things afresh – and with the benefit of hindsight – sets your mind free to explore alternative routes and pathways.

Entering the ice age

'Don't let life discourage you; everyone who got where he is had to begin where he was.'

RICHARD L. EVANS

As young children, we never had any reason to consider the issue of creativity; it wasn't a subject we were told to study. Our creative abilities became gradually more sophisticated simply through play and experimentation in a conducive environment. We were encouraged by responsible parents, and by others such as primary school teachers who understood the crucial importance of creative thinking and individual expression.

Of course, schools vary enormously in their approach to the fostering of individual expression, but however lofty their ambition in this regard is, it can become increasingly compromised in later years as the narrow confines of the school curriculum dictate the learning process and gradually eliminates freedom of expression.

The hibernation process truly sets in as creative thinking gradually gives way to a more rigid approach based on passing an increasing number of tests and examinations. Thinking in a different and questioning way is, if anything, discouraged. This may be no more sinister than the consequence of time constraints: there is often such a volume of work to get through that children asking questions simply cannot be accommodated.

Furthermore, we can only guess at the consequences for creativity of league tables and the publication of performance statistics, whatever merits these initiatives may have. Force-feeding students, so that they can simply regurgitate the facts and achieve the results the teachers and schools so desperately need, results in a vicious circle that can only damage the individual's capability for individual thought and expression. In too many instances, students are no longer allowed the time to digest information properly and question it, and there is therefore very little opportunity for them to get excited about anything; the red tape that teachers now have to deal with does not allow them to encourage that.

Only those who move on to higher education can expect any real degree of creative thinking to be re-introduced to the curriculum. The rest move on to seek their fortunes in the 'real' world. It is little wonder that many entrepreneurs get frustrated by the rigidity of the whole system and cannot wait to leave school at the earliest available opportunity and pursue a career, Bill Gates being a well-documented example.

The rigidity of the school curriculum is not the only destroyer of creative embers in children and young adults. Like parents, schoolteachers have an enormous responsibility to encourage children in anything for which they demonstrate a genuine enthusiasm. There will be many of a certain generation familiar with the consequences of ridicule, of failure to identify and encourage the unconventional, and in some cases just of downright bad teaching. Poor teachers may be in the minority but where they exist they can inflict long-lasting damage.

For those of us who can genuinely identify a poor teacher as being the root cause of a lack of enthusiasm for a given subject, the greatest legacy we can give is to remember that in all our dealings with others and help foster enthusiasm and creativity in all those that work for us.

For every casualty, there will be many more of us who have been inspired by teachers and can thank them in no small part for our successful careers. And as our skills and experience grow, we need to remember how influential our own behaviour can be and inspire our colleagues and employees accordingly.

Permafrost

'If I'd have gone to art school, or stayed in anthropology, I probably would have ended up back in film. . . . Mostly I just followed my inner feelings and passions . . . and kept going to where it got warmer and warmer, until it finally got hot. . . . Everybody has talent. It's just a matter of moving around until you've discovered what it is.'

GEORGE LUCAS

Perhaps the single biggest reason creativity goes into hibernation is that so many of us fail to find the career for which we are best suited. This is when our creative soul can go into a permanent hibernation, passionless and trapped underneath a creative permafrost.

Like settling for the wrong partner, when we adopt a career in which our interest is low, creative thought goes out of the window. While we may find ways to earn adequate remuneration, it is hardly the stuff of dreams and our quality of life will ultimately suffer – immeasurably. This is something we should all have learnt at school when it was clear how much of a struggle it was to excel at a subject that failed to excite us, so why should any of us think it would be different with our careers? If we have little interest in our job, or the products and services our businesses sell, how can we expect to contribute in a significant way?

Of course, the simple laws of economics dictate that we cannot all have the plum jobs, even if we have the ability. In the first few years of our careers, it is quite usual to engage in a variety of jobs, which in any case has the advantage of broadening our experience at the same time as giving us time to find our right vocation.

However, the economic necessity that often forces our hand early on can prevail for many years and in some cases for entire careers. Unfortunately, even though opportunities may arise throughout our lives to choose a line of work more in tune with our creative ability and preference, the perceived risks associated with such a change increase over time and are invariably considered too much to bear.

Although they seem to have much wider options, many professionals also follow career paths that have little or nothing to do with their natural inclinations. They choose them as a safe bet, a low risk option that is taken on the basis of availability, an attractive starting salary or simply to emulate the career path of one of their parents. If they had their time again, how many would chose a different career and follow a more creative path that excited genuine zeal and enthusiasm?

But heading into a vocational permafrost is not just a question of opportunity and chance; that would be a much too convenient explanation. Luck plays its part but so too does growing responsibility and, in particular, our attitude to risk. That is why the more risks we take early in our careers, when our financial and family responsibilities have not yet started to compromise our freedom of choice, the better. Like individuals, businesses too have to strike a balance between risk and reward, a judgement that has to be made on a daily basis. And although there is no single balance that is perfect – that will vary from one individual, company or sector to another – creativity cannot be expected to prosper in a climate of risk aversion.

If you find that your career is already in hibernation because you are in the wrong industry, company or department, you will need to take a long hard look at what drives you, where you want to get to and recognise that risks will need to be taken sooner or later.

Issues for family businesses

Given the enormous number of family-owned businesses throughout the world, we feel that this sector warrants particular attention. There are many such businesses that are renowned for their inventiveness and creativity. However, their unique characteristics, particularly the manner in which they pass down through successive generations, can often result in creativity being seriously stifled, even to the point of being completely snuffed out.

Nowhere is the pressure of following in the footsteps of a parent more acute than in the case of a family-owned business. Even where a parent takes the responsible position of allowing the next generation complete freedom of choice, the individual often feels a responsibility to join the business anyway, regardless of the extent of their passion for and belief in it.

It may seem an obvious statement, but it is absolutely essential to genuinely establish whether the succeeding generation inherits the same passion for the business. Very occasionally, the answer is black or white. However, a large number of people lie in the grey area in between: they are not yet sure. It is often an acute dilemma that is felt by everyone concerned, and honesty and communication, however uncomfortable, must be the guiding principles.

Whether a member of the succeeding generation is in that grey area or not, it is often wise to first extend one's academic career or to work in other industries, or do both, to ensure that the final decision to join the family business is made with a reasonable degree of maturity and experience. For many who go on to join the family business, there may never be another chance to broaden their experience of other businesses and cultures – invaluable reference points from which to judge and improve the family business. In any case, in our early years there are a great many other things to get passionate about; we live in a world of growing choice and distraction and it only seems prudent that these opportunities are adequately explored before a decision is made.

From the owner's perspective, the dilemma is also a very difficult one, and worsening as each decade passes by. If we are having children later and later in life, and those children are taking longer to decide on the right career path, how long should the owner have to wait to resolve the succession issue?

One thing is for sure: the aspirations and skills of each generation are rarely a perfect fit. The owner may choose to have some regard for the particular skills that the next generation seems to have, but this needs to tempered by the present need to run the business in a manner that achieves its goals, and to exercise the freedom to make any major structural changes that are deemed necessary. The competition is not going to wait idly by while the business makes up its mind about its future direction.

By the same token, if the succeeding generation has the skill, aptitude and enthusiasm to take the business on, sooner or later the successors will need to reshape the business according to *their* skills and enthusiasm in the style of the new management, not the old. They must have sufficient freedom to direct the business in their own way without the emotional baggage of feeling tied to the previous ways of doing things. A sentimental attachment to traditional activities and processes will be no match for the hard-nosed competition who will judge matters on their commercial merits alone.

While all decisions must be judged on commercial grounds, the freedom to choose is the greatest motivation that a new owner can experience, and the sooner this can be achieved the better. As with all things in life, the transition between the new and the old requires sound but sensitive judgement.

Indeed, the challenge for us all is to try to choose, or shape, a career that we are keenly interested in. Our quality of life will be enhanced immeasurably, a positive creative contribution will be made and, in all probability, financial reward will also be increased.

The challenge for the business is to find a strong balance of creative people doing the jobs that they are passionate about.

Rather surprisingly, and this is true of most businesses, success, or rather the complacency that often imperceptibly creeps along with it, can be another cause of creative hibernation.

Like our childhood, the early stages of a successful career or a business are characterised by high levels of energy and imagination. As success comes along, however, the temptation for a business to blindly stick to a winning formula and then sit back and enjoy the trappings of success quickly stifles creative thought, and complacency has no place in a thriving business.

A frequent cause of complacency in family-owned companies is lack of drive or hunger. This can arise for many reasons, including the accumulation of wealth that has not been earned by sufficient effort. When this is allied with lack of passion and a dwindling appreciation of the original ethos of the firm, dire consequences are inevitable. Competitors do not just replicate our best ideas; they advance them and use them against us. They stay leaner and get faster; they become predators that can sense a rotting corpse and will gladly feed on the remains. Equally critical is the fact that complacent businesses will neither retain nor attract the talented and creative staff that they so desperately need, and as these individuals gravitate towards the competition, the vicious circle of declining competitiveness gathers pace.

On the other hand, sticking blindly to a firm's original strategy regardless of the prevailing market conditions can put a family business in trouble faster than almost anything else. This has been seen time and again in manufacturing where a sentimental attachment to tradition and a reluctance to introduce the sweeping changes required quickly prove the company's undoing; dipping into the family silver to keep it afloat is no substitute for tough decision making, however unpalatable.

When vision and creativity lie dormant in an organisation for any significant length of time, it is heading for a very serious wake-up call. The damage caused is often so serious and deep-rooted that it cannot be repaired; even for the most successful firms this can result in a slow, painful decline and their ultimate demise.

Allow creativity to go into hibernation for too long and your business can start looking forward to the final stage in its evolution: extinction.

Coming out of the ice age: New Year's Day syndrome

For many of us, once in every year, without even trying too hard, there is a temporary thawing in our permafrost. It comes at a time when we have filled ourselves with good cheer and stoked our furnaces with all manner of calorific indulgences, allowing our icy exterior to melt just enough to allow new thoughts and ideas to enter inside. It follows a period of escape from the norm, a chance to stop for once and relax along with the rest of the population.

As we approach each New Year, a tiny part of our brains starts to prepare for a fresh start and a subtle but familiar sense of optimism starts to creep into our being. This annual phenomenon reaches its crescendo at midnight on New Year's Eve when we finally kiss goodbye to the old and embrace the new. It is a poignant moment when we reflect and look forward simultaneously. And despite the fact that many of us will be inebriated beyond the point of comprehension at that moment, we all still wake up the next day with a sense that somehow overnight things have changed, somehow things are going to be different.

But they rarely are.

On New Year's Day, we don't have to conjure up any new resolutions, we just use the ones from last year. Like the Christmas decorations that adorn our homes, we bring out our growing collection of resolutions, dust them off and present them to the world once more. The process has become a tradition, something we do almost out of habit, hardly anybody notices them. We trot out the usual pledges to earn more, re-ignite our careers, drink less, exercise girth control, take up a new hobby and so on.

Across the land, bars and clubs seem a little quieter, gymnasiums and swimming baths a little busier, while advertising takes on its seasonal complexion to take advantage of our new resolve. Unfortunately, much of this resolve is simply a shallow reaction to the excesses of the festive season: a knee-jerk reaction to an overdose of pies, chocolate, booze and indolence. All too often it does not last; one by one we drop our new commitments as habit, temptation and the rigours of everyday life steadily re-assert themselves and we are left exactly where we started, maybe a little fatter, perhaps a touch slower and still in the same job or department facing the same problems. The permafrost is back.

We call this temporary embracing of change and creative thinking New Year's Day syndrome.

The fact is that New Year's Day is just like a birthday – it is just a number – we are one day older that is all, nothing has changed, and neither have we.

But despite the apparent futility of the resolutions we make, at least we are making an effort. Our pledges demonstrate the fact that we are at least conscious of the need for change, to try something new or to take on a fresh challenge. And while most of us fail to reach our ultimate goal, we have nevertheless tried and we will be back to try again. Eventually, there is a chance that we will consolidate on the momentum of 1 January and go on to change our lives irrevocably, and for the better.

So New Year's Day syndrome is something of an affliction; it shows how easily our best intentions to carry out change and think more creatively get frozen before they have the chance to blossom. And yet, it is also a condition that hints at a way forward by reminding us that we are at least willing to stand back once in a while, look at our lives and try to do something about them.

In business, we also start a new calendar or financial year with a sense of optimism and an appetite for change, but all too quickly we find ourselves back on the hamster wheel. We need to learn how to reinvigorate our thinking by getting off that wheel on a regular basis, not just for a few days each year. To do that we need to know when we are running on it; we need to be able to recognise the symptoms early, identify why they occur and know what remedial action is required.

In the next two chapters we will look at ways in which we can escape from New Year's Day syndrome and make creative thinking and visioning a permanent part of our lives: ways in which we can keep our minds warm, open and receptive. We will look at the many factors that form a barrier to creative thinking and explore the ways in which these obstacles can be overcome, such as the ability to 'slide back into neutral' and the importance of regular holidays and high days. We will then take you through a comprehensive range of techniques to enable you clearly to identify your problems, set your goals and turn your newly envisioned future into reality. We will show you how to melt back the layers of ice that render us rigid in thought and movement, and how to become a truly creative thinker.

Annexe

The survey: creativity news from the frontline

To help prepare our thoughts for this book, we conducted research among a wide cross section of people for whom creativity plays an important part in their lives. In addition to people in the conventional business world, we drew our questionnaire mailing list from a wide selection of categories that we felt would willingly and effectively contribute to the debate: architects, designers, journalists, actors, creative directors, teachers and the occasional Nobel Laureate.

Our respondents were invited to answer a range of questions that we hoped would throw some light on how they and the world at large perceive the concept of creativity. The questions, and the answers we received, were as follows:

Question 1. What would be your definition of creativity?

Bearing in mind that we had to write a whole book on the subject before we could arrive at a definition that we felt was vaguely useful, we were perhaps lucky that our first question did not put more people off. It is to the immense credit of our respondents that, despite this almost impossible opener, they attempted to answer it and then doggedly persisted with the rest of the questionnaire. Asking for a definition of the meaning of life would hardly have been any more difficult. Nevertheless, certain threads of thought became clear as we studied the responses.

Many felt the essence of creativity was simply the forming of thoughts and ideas, whether new or old, and that by looking at them from a new perspective, fresh solutions could be found. Several identified spontaneity, or at least the ability to seize and act upon its results, as another key ingredient of the process.

The ability to move beyond the known was seen as a pre-requisite to creative thinking. Martin Elliott, a singer, defined creativity as 'when there are no boundaries mentally to what one might conceive to be possible', and Andrea McLean, a journalist and presenter, characterized it as 'using your imagination to go beyond the obvious'. One intriguing suggestion by the architect Lawrence A. Gage was that creativity is the ability to respond 'positively to the world "as it is" rather than how others would have us believe'.

Significantly, many considered that any true definition of creativity needed to reflect the need either to improve the society in which we live or, as head teacher Dr Colin H. R. Niven states, to 'benefit mankind as a whole or at least a small community or individual'.

But despite some bold attempts to provide a single definition, it was clear from the responses that the essence of creativity is very much for individuals to define for themselves according to their own sensibilities, interests and field of work. For many, understandably, a single definition was not possible and Eric Smith, a designer, summed up what appeared to be on the minds of a number of respondents when he acknowledged that 'I cannot define creativity – one is born with it; how it develops is the measure of greatness but I cannot explain creativity'.

Question 2. Who is the most creative person you can think of and why?

The whole spectrum was covered from God ('who else could have created such beauty and awesomeness and inspired us to wonder' mused Mike Le-Worthy, a head teacher) to 'my friend Bob' (a graphic designer known to Stuart Turner, also a head teacher, who regards some of his work as 'really different'). Jesus Christ was singled out for offering 'new ways of creative living, none of which have yet been fully tried out, but which could genuinely prevent conflict and hatred'.

Leonardo da Vinci was a popular choice, described by one respondent as the complete creator: 'creative in both artistic matters and practical ones, his war machines, submarines, helicopters etc., not to mention his poetry, painting, drawing and architecture'. Bridget O'Connor, a headmistress, wrote that da Vinci 'wanted to look at the new, and was not afraid of challenging assumptions; he wanted practical implications, but drew on lessons from the past and combined art and beauty with practicality'.

Picasso was chosen by Tom Bevan, a car designer, because of his 'original way of translating an idea or thought from mind to canvas', and several respondents considered Thomas Edison to be the most creative person, invariably citing his '99 per cent perspiration, 1 per cent inspiration' maxim.

The enormous variety of responses, particularly in the way that working partners or friends were often chosen in preference to your average genius, illustrates how much inspiration can be, and is, drawn from those in our immediate acqaintance.

Question 3. Which is the most creative company you can think of and why?

Many of the companies that are commonly cited as creative were listed including Benetton, which according to Lori Baldwin is 'not afraid to shock', whilst retaining a certain 'beauty and dynamic approach' and Bridget O'Connor who singled out Ben & Jerry's because it 're-wrote the rules of a complete enterprise'. Other companies that were noted include The Body Shop, Apple, Gaggia and IKEA.

Interestingly, a number of people felt that no company could be described as inherently creative. At the very least, they felt that the notion required qualification. Val Palmer, a course director in graphic and industrial design, considered the question to be a 'tricky one', saying that 'companies aren't creative – it's individuals or groups of individuals who are creative; finding the right combination is the key'. Martin Elliott went even further, to say that 'a company by definition is not creative because it has already formed limitations by grouping itself together under rules and regulations set by others'.

While we do believe that companies *can* be regarded as creative in 'themselves', we very much take on board these important qualifications. First, businesses are largely the product of the people that work for them, and if they are to be looked upon as truly creative, then creative thinking needs to permeate through the entire organisation not simply exist in the odd pocket here and there, or confined to senior management. Second, companies are being subjected to an increasing weight of rules, regulations and red tape which, when combined with the short-term needs of survival or satisfying hungry shareholders, can result in creativity being completely driven out, whatever their original ethos, with potentially devastating implications for their longer term future.

Question 4. Do you think it is possible to improve your creative thinking and how?

Whilst the methods suggested varied considerably, there was a unified and positive response to the first part of the question: yes.

Many believe that it is vital that the process of sharpening our creative ability should start very early on in our lives. Lucy Meacock, a presenter, considers that 'creative thinking needs encouraging from above' and poignantly, adds the observation that 'every young child can paint – until a teacher or parent tells them that they can't'. By the same token, she also makes the point that, 'once you are told that you have a good idea it's amazing how many more you have'. Mike Le-Worthy also identified 'encouragement and the building of self-esteem as being crucial to the development of creative powers', and he too stressed the importance of this process starting at an early age.

Although Dr Colin Niven felt that there was probably an absolute limit to which an individual's creative thinking could be improved, he identified practice as being crucial: 'writers, painters, engineers, doctors all get better with practice, trial and error and experimentation' he suggested. Val Palmer agreed that creativity was a skill that could be learnt through practice and by being receptive to those around us, 'by observing how others do it, again and again – laborious, but it works' she asserted. Lucy Meacock concurred by suggesting that we should surround ourselves with creative people and keep an open mind. 'When something catches your attention, ask yourself, why did it stand out? Try looking at a subject from a completely different angle by putting yourself in someone else's shoes.'

A number of people felt that providing the right environment and culture was crucial in stimulating creative thought. According to Brook Banham, 'it is possible to be more creative if you allow yourself to "free up" your mind. It's about opening your subconscious thoughts coupled with an ability to depict or illustrate those thoughts.' He believes that 'everyone has the potential to be creative, though some people have turned off the creative part of their consciousness for so long, it would be difficult to get it active again', an inert state we refer to as creative hibernation, which in its extreme form might be referred to as a kind of permafrost.

One or two of our respondents even went so far as to suggest the smoking of marijuana. Although in certain parts of the world the sharing of a 'smoke' may be an essential part of many problem-solving management meetings – much like a Native American pow-wow – we are somewhat reluctant to recommend this as a creative technique. That being said, when one considers the creative contributions made by poets such as Samuel Taylor Coleridge and artists such as Lennon and McCartney, we sort of know what our respondees are driving at.

Andrea McLean had a simple recommendation: 'Go on holiday!' The best ideas, she proposes, 'always happen when you're relaxed and thinking about nothing in particular'. The notion of creation through recreation is a theme that runs through this book and, like Ms McLean, we regard vacations from the norm as an essential means of providing the climate for spontaneous creativity.

But perhaps the most striking of all the opinions offered was that of Lawrence Gage who, while agreeing with everyone else that it is possible to improve creative thinking – in his view 'by learning from nature, our best teacher' – challenges us to 'forget "originality" – it is nothing but human conceit'.

Food for thought indeed!

Question 5. What is your approach to using creativity to solve problems?

The vast majority of respondents identified teamwork and brainstorming as crucial means of solving problems. Lori Baldwin, an interior designer, stated the importance of involving 'more that one person in the process, to carefully evaluate their input and to then filter the ideas through to conclusion'. Mike Le-Worthy also expressed the need to value the ideas of others, particularly in encouraging those people to come forward with ideas. Significantly, he adds that we need to appreciate that 'very few people have the ability to create a solution and see it through; some are good at starting, for others to complete'.

Most people also recommended a pragmatic, cyclical approach. Val Palmer recommends that if the 'spontaneous solution doesn't happen, then a methodical trawl through the facts (with or without accomplices)' is required, 'followed by a period of reflection, then do it all again'. Lawrence Gage follows a similar theme: 'analysis – brainstorming – appraisal – reduction to a basic, simple idea – reinforcement'. 'Detailed development' he continues, 'should flow naturally from the basic idea . . . if it does not, it's back to the beginning'.

Bridget O'Connor made both points in her response by recommending a cycle of 'reflection, brainstorming and meditation' and adding that 'resourcing and networking are crucial' to any creative solution.

Using imagination was another key point: 'Dream of things that never were and ask "why not?"' suggested Ian M. Small, a headteacher, while Martin Elliott recommends that we 'think of a solution and then check the absolute opposite'. Dr Colin Niven's technique is to 'try to visualise an ideal outcome and work towards it – shafts of intelligence suddenly suggest other outcomes'.

But invaluable as problem-solving techniques are – and we'll be suggesting quite a few in later chapters – creative thinking is often simply born out of necessity, and so we conclude our review of creative approaches with the words of Andrea McLean who wrote: 'I have a three month old baby, so I'm always being creative in solving problems! Problems with crying, teething, sleeping you name it. Basically, if it pops into my head I try it, and if it works – brilliant!'

Question 6. Which nationality do you think is the most creative and why?

Arguably, this question provoked the strongest response, with some people at a complete loss as to why we asked it at all, as was evidenced by the sudden preponderance of indignant exclamation marks in their responses. Their comments ranged from Lori Baldwin's 'I think this concept is rubbish (sorry!)', Bridget O'Connor's 'absolutely not PC –

is this a *just* question?' to Ian Small's 'Silly question! Creativity has nothing to do with nationality, but to do with environment. A poor Tunisian might be truly creative in making a home, a greater achievement for him than Microsoft for Mr. Gates'. Lawrence Gage too, considers nationality to be 'irrelevant', going on to say that '"necessity being the mother of invention" – the third world countries have a more creative attitude to life and business, sometimes to the dismay of the western world, bound by our blinkered conventions'.

We are grateful for these forthright comments since we see them as entirely consistent with, and reinforcing, our own belief in the universality of creativity. Certainly this was a point made by the majority, although many agreed with Ian Small's observation and qualified their views accordingly. For Dr Colin Niven, it is not so much a question of nationality as of opportunity, while Lucy Meacock is more specific in identifying lack of resources as a common differential.

Equally, we are thankful to those who did identify certain nationalities as being more 'creative', particularly since they invariably made the point, like Dr Niven, that a nation's creative pool of resources was in large part a reflection of opportunity, government policy on working conditions, research and development, the work–life balance, social tolerance and reward. Geoff Crook, a course director in graphic and industrial design, summed up this position by observing that 'everyone can be creative, there are no genetic advantages, just different cultural criteria'.

But the final words on this subject are to go to Martin Elliott who states quite simply, that 'creativity belongs to individuals not nations'.

Question 7. Has some creative thinking ever made a big difference to your life?

While the responses to the questionnaire were all in the affirmitive, we can think of no better way to conclude our review of the survey than to simply use Bridget O'Connor's closing words:

> Massive! Sometimes creative thinking has made life less easy, but the essence of creative thinking is to go on believing in it. As an

educator, I firmly believe that we owe it to youngsters to give them the environment – including the thrills, spills and safety nets – to enjoy the positive power of creativity.

Inspired by these words of wisdom, we set about writing this book, which aims to help people who, like Bridget O'Connor, want to enjoy the thrills and spills of the journey towards improved creativity.

CHAPTER 3

Starting the creativity flow

Getting started

There are surely very few people, no matter how spiritually or finan-
cially secure, who do not wish to keep improving or modifying
aspects of their lives. We are all looking for solutions to knotty problems. For many of us, the solution comes after some thought is
applied. But all too often, we get stuck in a rut: unable to move
forward, constantly procrastinating over a dilemma or simply
pondering the years away, without tackling problems or fulfilling
dreams.

Our competitors keep moving ahead and others increasingly enjoy
the recognition that used to be ours. The new product pipeline dries
up, efficiency deteriorates, costs soar and service levels plunge.

The cost in financial loss, personal stress and suffering can be high
if we find ourselves in a position where innovative thinking has
evaporated and all new ideas and useful thought begin to vanish.
After a while, obstacles come to dominate objectives and we can
start to lose perspective and the hope of finding solutions.

When problems seem insurmountable, we try all sorts of means
and ways to change our state. We might think about what we would
like to do and sit staring into space. We try reading self-help books,
organising brainstorms at work, setting up subgroups and commit-
tees and talking long into the night in the hope that some magic
bullet will come along.

But the truth is that we usually remain stuck and the problem is
simply rolled forward like a heavy stone to be carried another day.

Sometimes we do not even try to change our fate. Everything
seems too daunting; we feel we just do not have time, or that any
ideas we have would never work, or would cost too much. Often we
simply feel that we do not know where to begin. You hear people

saying things like: 'it has all been done before' or lamenting that there is no way round something.

This feeling of despair is often reinforced and echoed by the negative voices of others. Those doom-laden calls are often very loud and the nay-sayers seem on occasion to relish the destruction of hope and optimism. You will be told that your idea has been tried before with disastrous consequences. You will be assured that your plan won't work, that you are being unrealistic to expect to change things and to succeed. There will be no shortage of pundits explaining that it is always far safer to do nothing or simply carry on doing what you are doing now and to be grateful. The truth of course is that it is madness to carry on doing the same thing and expect different results.

Often we cope through denial. We kid ourselves that everything is fine. We ignore warning signs or cheat ourselves by lowering our own standards and goals. We compare ourselves with others in a way that makes us feel less badly off. We tell ourselves that things could be worse.

This self-delusion is corrosive and withering, leaving us eternally hoping that everything will be fine and work out for the best, yet not actually doing anything to grasp control of your fate and influence your destiny. We call this 'lottery players' syndrome'. This mind-set sees people buying lottery tickets and scratch cards week after week, in the hope that their fortunes will be turned around by fate rather than through their own application and efforts.

Even worse is when we do not even know what we are missing. When this is the case, we deny ourselves even the opportunity to dream about how things could be better, how we could be more fulfilled, less bored or more willing to get out of bed every morning. We are not equipped to imagine a different way and as a result we never have the chance to catch a glimpse of that better world, of improved results, of that promotion, or achieving our dreams.

It is not that we do not see a way to reach our goals; this state of mind is far graver than that. Our dreams are not just out of reach; we have not even begun to think about what our dreams could be.

All this lack of direction and focus can lead to a great deal of unhappiness. Unfulfilled aspirations through the torpor of human nature and an ossified imagination are at the root of much of the depression and unease in society. Time passes and the next thing you know, your business competitors have killed you off, or your whole market has changed because someone has invented something that makes your business virtually obsolete.

Whatever the wake-up call, when it happens you will run the risk of finding you have run out of time, are bereft of ideas and bitterly disappointed. But it is never too late to act. If you apply yourself now, you can turn around your problems and can do what you want to do. Even if you do not get all the way, you can at least derive a sense of satisfaction through striving and taking a greater degree of control over your own progress and fate. Although your may think the creativity boat has left you behind, it is never too late to start applying creativity to help solve your problems and drive change in your business.

Hurdles to creative thinking and problem solving

There can be many reasons why we fail to address and solve our problems at work. A key first step to finding solutions is to recognise the nature of potential obstacles. Only then will we have any chance of approaching a problem in a way that is likely to succeed. Later on we will look at ways of solving problems through a variety of creative techniques.

But before that, it is worth considering some of the typical obstacles to creative thought that you might encounter. In this section, we examine each type of obstacle and consider approaches to dissolve the psychological dams that clog the flow of thought and innovation.

The obstacles we will look at are as follows:

■ fear

■ perfectionism

■ complacency

■ lack of time

■ not seeing the real issue

- one-dimensional thinking

- a negative atmosphere and environment.

Fear

Although we can be very clear that we want things to change, we are often afraid of making any move to alter the situation. We can be afraid of many things that freeze us in a trance of indecision. We may fear even to scratch the surface of a problem lest it stir up unpleasant conflict or debate. Often we prefer to leave things as they are rather than risk unsettling the status quo.

We can also be strongly discouraged by the thought that if we try to change things, we might fail. This can lead to an apathy and conservatism in outlook that rarely generates any effective strategies.

Sometimes we dare to think slightly differently, but fight shy of really thinking big enough. Our comfort zone only allows us to think incrementally, taking us to the next minor step forward. We strive for the adequate. Yet if we are planning to launch a new business or trying a different approach to reach the market, why not aim really high from the start? Most of us think it almost laughable that we could be the 'industry leader' or the 'world's largest', or the 'best selling' of whatever it is we are contemplating. Yet why should this not be so?

The world's biggest corporations were all once small start-ups. The difference – or at least one of the key differences – between the firms that today dominate corporate life and smaller enterprises that have not grown to such a size, is often the vision and desire of the founders to be one of the world's leading firms in their industries.

What is it that makes one entrepreneur, starting with one restaurant, turn that into a worldwide chain and another spend an entire career with a single property? True, in many cases the single outlet will be the desired goal for an individual, but many others simply do not have the conviction or the self-confidence to think in terms of greater scale. They have ambitions, but deep down they believe that growth of that order is 'not for them'. But the real question is: 'why not?'

Often the only thing separating the single site operator from the multi-site chain, is the desire and self-confidence to keep on expanding. It is the lack of fear – the sheer self-belief – that allows certain business people to see endless opportunities while others shy away, seeing only the negative possibilities.

Another common source of fear is a terror of change and of having to put in place new ways of doing things. It is one thing being happy with the way things are and not wanting to change, but it is entirely different if the current situation is not satisfactory and yet there is still fear and reluctance to do anything about it.

Fear of change is often very deep rooted and can be difficult to comprehend and no less difficult to deal with. Probably one of the simplest ways of considering how easy change can be is to reflect on times when it has been imposed – perhaps by redundancy or an accident – or has occurred naturally, such as through moving house or taking a new job.

With such events behind us, it is reassuring to remind ourselves that we are still here, that the world did not, in fact, come to an end and that in many cases the modification to the past regime was actually an improvement.

Sometimes we need to look back to give ourselves the confidence to go forward.

It is by taking this hindsight view of change and seeing that it was not so bad after all, that we can help educate ourselves to recognise that change is certainly not always dire and quite often it can be rather rewarding.

Many people tend to be afraid of moving beyond the known world of their experience. As children, we are constantly encouraged by adults to try new things and our comfort zone steadily expands as a result of that combined with our own sense of curiosity. But how many parents who encourage this are leading by example? If anything, most adults are trapped in a *shrinking* comfort zone. This can be a real constraint to business and professional development.

Clearly not every foray into new territory will be successful. Mistakes – if that is the right word – are inevitable. The negative consequences of change could range from boredom to some degree of financial or career setback. However, it is unlikely that the experience will be entirely without reward. Even if it establishes clearly what not to do in the future, then that alone will have been a valuable lesson. Who knows what other pieces of information of self-knowledge will be gleaned along the way, which can then be applied to future endeavours?

In fact, many successful people make mistakes; it is all part of the learning process, and in many ways it is what defines them. They experiment early in their careers, they are bold in their thoughts and actions, and as a result their learning curves are very much steeper than the average person's. There is no faster way to learn than from a mistake, and the bigger it is the greater the lesson. With a steep learning curve, mistakes only cause temporary setbacks; the successful entrepreneur will always bounce back stronger and wiser.

Besides, for every less successful brush with change, there will be many more successful experiences where we will supplement our knowledge and experience in ways that greatly advantage our prospects. Our research indicates that the key to minimising 'change pains' is to avoid viewing each foray and move as 'the final frontier'.

All too often we see a move as being the last one we will want to make. If this works, we argue, then that will be it. However, putting all our hopes into one basket in this way is a risk-all strategy that allows little room for manoeuvre.

Far better to see each move as a step on a long but rewarding journey. That way we are more likely to approach change in a much more positive, less fearful way. Each decision – while clearly important – will be less charged with that high sense of drama that comes from seeing each significant change as the definitive move in our careers or businesses.

The journey can be likened to the progress of a rambler who walks along undulating terrain with its ups and downs but steadily ascends the heights. At various stages our explorer can look back at the journey achieved, and from the increased altitude form a clearer vision of the world. This contrasts sharply with those who see change as something that exists beyond the edge of a cliff.

The key to making lots of improvements is to have lots of ideas. The more change we throw against a wall, the more that is likely to stick. As we practice handling different situations, or trying new things, we become more comfortable and better at understanding how to shape events to our advantage.

Humans are remarkable in the way they can cope with changes in circumstances and altered events. The human sprit – if kept positive – will adapt to make the most of transformed circumstances. If we allow it, we can cope with adjustment, and assimilate new situations into our everyday lives with remarkable ease. Once we have decided to try new things, it is surprising to look back after a short while and see how commonplace and easy our new ways have become. Something that seemed difficult, unfamiliar and frightening when we first started it, now – looking back – seems simple and modest. Surely every one of us who can drive a car will remember those first few hours behind the wheel trying to master the controls. At the time, the prospect of co-ordinating feet and hands, checking the mirror, signalling, steering and being aware of the road seemed terrifying and surely beyond the abilities of any average human. Looking back now, when driving is second nature, we can hardly believe that this everyday activity was once a seemingly impossible challenge.

Reminding ourselves of where we once were when we started to tackle any challenge, and then looking at how far we have come, is a powerful tool in overcoming fear and achieving change in our lives. By reflecting on occasions where we have overcome challenges, celebrating our achievements and analysing our past behaviour and approaches, we can draw sufficient confidence to tackle new problems.

Perfectionism

On first consideration, the desire to strive for a perfect outcome might not appear to be much of a blocker to the creative process. In fact, it can be one of the most serious barriers, not only to creative thinking but also to overall performance and productivity, and ultimately to career and business progression.

Perfectionists typically find it difficult to apply the 80/20 rule and the law of diminishing returns to their own tasks and activities. With the exception of financial reporting and some highly technical areas, the number of times that a 100 per cent solution is required is very rare, and indeed it is often unattainable. More often than not, the timely arrival of an 80–90 per cent solution is far better than a 100 per cent solution that takes much longer to produce. The irony is that the 100 per cent solution is often worthless.

We sum this up with our 5-P Rule: Punctual Pragmatism always beats the Poor Performance of Perfectionism. Perfectionism is closely related to fear as a blocker to creativity. It is often rooted in our early schooldays when the desire to produce excellent, near-perfect work is frequently deemed an attribute. We have already looked at how free thinking can gradually make way to a narrower form as we progress through our education. Perfectionists can be particularly prone to this failure to tap into their creative potential, and once ingrained, perfectionism is a very difficult habit to shake off.

Fastidiousness manifests itself in an acute fear of failure and of imperfection; perfectionists fear mistakes and tend to be strongly adverse to risk. There is always a role for perfectionists, but when it comes to the free flow of ideas and brainstorming, perfectionism can get in the way.

Managers need to take care that a culture of perfectionism does not overwhelm a business. It is important to understand where we can afford to tolerate this trait and where it could be destructive. Otherwise, there is a risk of being left in the wake of our more pragmatic competitors who encourage new ideas, make speedy decisions and who are not adverse to the odd mistake.

Complacency

While fear can have a crippling effect on change and innovative thinking, it can often be easily overcome with some positive thinking. Those who fear change are in one way fortunate as they are starting from a position that is by its nature uncomfortable: being afraid can be a negative driver. The fact that they are starting from an undesirable situation, means that they are more likely to want to get out of the hole and move on.

However, perhaps a far more serious blocker to creative thinking and to innovation in general is complacency and overconfidence. Contemplating change when everything appears to be going well is, for many, a counter-intuitive thought process. The mind-set is all too often: if everything is going well, why tinker with it. 'If it ain't broke, don't fix it' is a cliché frequently heard in modern business. A better approach would be: 'it ain't broke, but let's see if it needs breaking'.

Complacency rarely occurs overnight; if it did, we would all spot it and take action. In reality, it starts off in a much milder form and then grows imperceptibly until real structural damage is done. Often the damage caused is so considerable that it cannot be repaired.

It is true that if something is going well, then there is no point in simply changing it for change's sake. This however does not stop those managers who take the view that 'if it ain't broke, then break it'. These individuals will, as a matter of principle, seek to change whatever is the status quo.

Often this desire to sweep the board clean is triggered when a new senior manager moves into a position. Often the new manager will have been given the post to replace a failing leader, so there may be a real need for change, but all too often the revolution is ego fuelled, with the incoming leader wishing to expunge all traces of the past and re-invent everything in his or her image.

While this type of arbitrary, random change may or may not be effective or even necessary, it is perhaps far less damaging than the other extreme which is studiously to seek to set the entire business in aspic, on the basis that it is running at its optimal level and therefore if it can simply carry on like this forever, then everything will be just fine.

Leaders of successful businesses who seek to preserve them in this way are often the architects of the destruction of the very thing they are seeking to protect. Because the truth is that things never can be frozen in time and space. Even if you succeed in suspending time within your own firm, the rest of the world moves on, catches up and rapidly overtakes you. Your own people become bored and stagnate, and the upward curve of success soon risks levelling out to a flat line.

The problem develops when success breeds complacency. The dangerous thought pattern is: 'why change if everything is going great?' This is – to an extent – understandable. If the profits are coming in and the business is leading its sector, surely it has 'made it'. What is the point of going any further and looking for change that is not needed?

This line of thought often leads to corporate cultures that exhibit the following:

■ *Loss of focus on the consumer.* A good example is the UK Conservative party, which dominated political life in the 1980s under Margaret Thatcher. Success was so consummate that the party felt it was invincible and stopped listening and responding to the public. When it came, the decline was rapid and the Tories spectacularly lost their mandate to rule.

■ *A 'yes' culture.* Highly successful firms often operate in a culture where any challenge to the status quo is strongly discouraged. It is as if there is a terror of breaking the magic spell that has given the organisation its success. It is perhaps a paradox that management teams are at their least critical in times of great success, often displaying highly compliant behaviour, which can be stifling and lethal for the long-term health of the business.

■ *Extreme isolation.* This can be seen in three main areas:
 – Attitudes to customers. When it comes to customers, highly successful firms often forget some of the basic rules of service. Often they feel that they are doing their customers a favour by selling to them and that the customers cannot afford to be without their product or service.
 – Attitudes to staff. Highly successful firms often begin to see staff as people who should be grateful for the opportunity to work there and who should also adapt totally to the successful ways of the organisation, without question or challenge.
 – Attitudes to other stakeholders. Similarly high-handed attitudes can develop towards suppliers, who are treated with disdain, rather than being recognised as key partners in the success of the firm. Other stakeholders too often suffer from organisational arrogance. Trade bodies, local communities, opinion formers, regulators, pressure groups and the media often are ignored or patronised by highly successful firms. The business often perceives itself as so successful that it does not need to engage with these groups. However, while that may be true for the moment, such arrogance leaves no goodwill in the bank, so that when these stakeholders are needed – perhaps at a time of crisis – there is no credit in the account to draw upon.

The truth is that many successful firms are at the top of a curve and the only way forward is down the other side of the roller coaster. This does not have to be the case, but all too often it is. Once success is attained, we often find it difficult to remember the lessons and fundamental principles that enabled us to succeed in the first place. The dedication to customer service, the restless pursuit for the improvement that leads to market success, are just two of the essentials of business life that are all too often abandoned once the goal has been attained. It should be remembered that our own success was often achieved by systematically setting out to destroy market leaders, or at least to outpace the number one position holders.

Although a firm may be winning now, there should be no doubt that others are racing to catch up and beat whatever the leader is up to. If we learn anything from business history, it should be that apparent leaders can be and are toppled with great frequency. It is well documented how few firms in the major financial listings are still around after 10 or 15 years. Companies that appear unstoppable disappear completely or fall way behind the competition and lose their dominant position with alarming regularity.

Yet at the time, the prospect that one day they could be nothing seems hard for many of these firms to contemplate seriously. However, a brief thought about the many once great firms that are now history, should soon bring any conceited executive back down to earth.

One technique used by some organisations to consider possible threats, is to set up a small hit squad that can look at a problem afresh, free, to a large extent, from baggage and vested interests.

This technique was famously employed by Jack Welch when he was running General Electric (GE) – the world's most valuable company; Welch took a group of younger executives and asked them to set up an anti-GE virtual firm called destroyyourbusiness.com. The idea was that the group should think about everything they would do as a competitor to GE to destroy it, as well as every possible external factor that could harm GE. For months they thought like competitors, studied social, political, technological and economic trends, and developed ideas, scenarios and plans that would take GE apart: stealing customers, disrupting trade, threatening every aspect of the GE empire and doing everything they could to bring the world's biggest company to its knees.

The purpose was to highlight GE's vulnerable points. Only by taking on the mind-set and posture of a competitor or an enemy could GE employees really see – in many cases for the first time – where their true weaknesses lay. The exercise also highlighted opportunities that GE was currently not exploiting. As a result of the initiative, GE developed many new creative ideas and ways of improving its businesses and making it even better protected from harm.

A similar approach was taken by British Airways, which faced growing competitive threats from low-cost airlines and a need to develop new profitable routes. The Chief Executive, Rod Eddington, took a cross-department team made up of representatives of BA from around the world, and set them the task of developing a no-holds-barred critique of the business and a plan for the future, where nothing was sacred. Eddington asked the group to think the unthinkable, to be brave, and spare nothing and nobody in its recommendations.

The liberating combination of having the time to work on these issues, support from the top and encouragement to think from the ground up were clearly key ingredients in both the BA and the GE examples and made significant contributions to the effectiveness of both working groups.

All too often, however, such doomsday scenario planning is not applied when a company is riding high. Imagine if you could go back in a time machine and tell the board of Marks and Spencer ten years ago that soon their business would be a laughing stock and on its knees: they would have thought your prognosis was idiotic. However some exploratory planning sessions on the threats at that time could have made a significant difference and made their recovery easier.

Think of all the businesses before the invention of the motor car, involved in making horse carriages, saddles and various paraphernalia for the thousands of these animals that had for centuries been a vital part of everyday life. If you had said to them that one day there will be an invention – the car – that will see the end of the horse as a significant means of transport, they would not have believed it for one moment.

People often find it very difficult to take themselves out of the present and imagine an alternative future. Our view of the future is typically based on extrapolations of the present or the past. Also, we get caught up in fashionable thinking and begin to accept conventional wisdom as somehow 'the truth' and feel afraid to challenge it in any way.

This was vividly seen in the dot.com bubble, when to question the claim that the Internet would change the world forever was to risk looking like a Luddite and appearing out of touch. The fervour of fashionable thought is self-perpetuating; as the snowball builds, it increasingly appears that to disagree is commercial suicide, even if deep down you simply do not believe everything you are hearing or seeing.

The human struggle to imagine a situation other than the one we are currently in is fundamental to why creative thought eludes so many of us. It affects virtually all our decisions. For example, when it is cold, it is hard to imagine what it is like when it is hot. We find it difficult to buy an umbrella on a dry day, even if we know that when it rains, umbrellas may cost more and be hard to find, and that we will get wet until we have one.

Millions of people do not have sufficient insurance cover or plans to protect themselves against unforeseen events, because they cannot imagine such occurrences happening to them despite statistics showing levels of probability that are quite high. History teaches us over and over again that the world changes; what seemed permanent is swept away and that which was once incontrovertibly dominant is usurped and becomes powerless and outdated.

Despite this evidence, most of us cannot see that this type of change in our own lives and businesses is not just possible but highly likely. People who can think creatively and introduce innovative new ways into their lives are free from the mental trap of the present. They can imagine different futures, different ways of living or working and of tackling existing situations.

Most of us find this difficult at the best of times, but those of us who are bound up in successful organisations will find it even harder than most. The confidence of victory binds the imagination and hold us in check.

Successful companies have no exemption from the need for creative thinking. Creativity is most probably one of the key reasons why they were successful in the first place, and they should never rest. They should never accept that they have reached their goal. They should understand that standing still is not an option. They should be forever searching for ways to replicate their success, planning to improve continuously their ways of working, brooding over what the competition is doing and how to keep outwitting them. Success is a terrific platform for even more improvement; it should not become a comfortable bed for self-satisfied sloth.

In Chapter 6 we will look at some creative techniques that work well with highly successful organisations, forcing such firms to imagine a less successful scenario and to consider what they would need to do to survive. Often this new perspective throws fresh light on complacent situations and indicates ways forward towards even greater success.

However, it is essential that there is a will to explore change and innovation, and any organisation that feels it is beyond improvement, should recognise that thought as a very worrying sign that complacency and arrogance are creeping in and must be banished as soon as possible.

Lack of time

While most of the hurdles we are looking at here are manufactured in our own heads and hearts, there is one obstacle – or apparent obstacle – to creativity that at first sight seems to be beyond our control, and that is available time. One thing we cannot change is the number of hours in a day. Lack of time to try anything new – to think of alternative approaches or to spend the extra hours needed to try and adopt new ways of working – is probably one of the most frequently cited reasons for not resolving problems or achieving the improvements that we all seek.

We end up in a vicious circle: how many of us have often thought about enrolling on a time management course only to discover that we cannot find the time? The key to resolving this problem lies in finding ways to break this cycle.

There is no doubt that lack of time can be a serious inhibiter of creativity. Also it is true that today there are ever-increasing pressures on our time. At least, there is a heightened perception that there is more pressure on our time. Perhaps it is more the case that we have higher expectations of the number of things that we feel can be achieved within set time periods. Many people seem almost to want to ignore time itself, and instead aim to complete an infinite number of tasks regardless of the finite time available.

There is also an undoubted and growing fear of not filling every moment of time with activity. Even children today are finding their parents cramming the day with scheduled events and activities that leave little or no time for simply relaxing, playing and 'doing nothing'.

If a moment in time is not allocated to some task or activity, it seems that we often become very anxious, equating free time with wasted time. This encourages us to build more and more into our days, trying to achieve an ever-higher quantity of tasks while the number of hours in the day remains the same.

We try to cheat time by working through holidays and weekends, sleeping less, getting up early or working late to 'buy time'. The consequence is high levels of sleep deprivation and exhaustion in our western societies. The impact on health and performance is still being quantified, but is proven to be detrimental to safety, well-being and to happiness.

There are many more demands on our time derived from new technology. Today we have to deal with so many more devices of communication – e-mails, pagers, PDAs and text messages – all of which have succeeded in gaining attention in our already crowded environments. There are more distractions – computer games, a greater range of leisure activities, hobbies, different ways of seeking entertainment, more restaurants, more films, more disposable income – just more of everything.

And we are not – yet – good at saying no. We lack the ability to discern the wheat from the chaff in this ever-growing range of options. Humans do not find self-denial easy. As we attain plenty in everything around us, our natural urge is to increase consumption accordingly. It is a deep-seated survivalist drive to gather now for fear of deprivation later, which sees us consuming beyond our needs as supply rises.

In the case of the obesity problem facing much of the Western world, the outcome of over-consumption is clear to see in the size of our bodies. We find it extremely hard to control our urge to keep feeding ourselves, even though food is far from scare any more. Similarly we stuff our hours and our minds with ever more sources of information and ever more activities, even though time remains constant. Even though we experience a diminishing sense of satisfaction and enlightenment, we rush from one frantic, shallow moment to another.

It can often seem as if there is no time to think. Either we are too busy dealing with the e-mails or the pressures of everyday life, or we are too exhausted by commuting, travelling and the relentless compression of timetables for delivery.

This feeling that there are not enough hours in the day for current things, let alone anything new, is a very common inhibitor to creativity that we come across in our work. It appears to be insurmountable due to the fact that there can never be more hours in a day. However, this is in reality just another artificial constraint we put upon ourselves. True, time is finite, but how we use that time is not. The key to managing time is to be clear about priorities and to allocate our use of this resource accordingly.

This can mean doing fewer things but insisting on doing those things that will lead to changes. There are a few non-negotiables around your time: sleep, eating and, in the long term, earning a living. However there are many other things that you do with your time that *are* negotiable. They can be traded – albeit temporarily – for other activities that you need to complete in order to achieve your goals. The key is being very clear about what you want, then being determined to carve out the time needed to achieve those things, and then building that new approach into your day. This brings us to probably the most important part of creative problem solving, which is correctly identifying the real need behind the creative challenge.

Not seeing the real issue

Often our problems seem unbeatable, because they are. Or rather, the problem as it is presented cannot be solved, because we are looking at the wrong problem or we are looking at the problem from an erroneous point of view.

For example, if we feel the problem is that 'there are not enough hours in a day', then the fact is that it is true. The number of hours in a day will not increase and therefore if we need extra hours to get things done it is indeed an impossible problem as new hours cannot – no matter how determined we are – be conjured out of thin air. We rapidly reach this conclusion, become disheartened and abandon hope.

However, this is an example of where we are mistakenly focusing on the wrong problem. The real issue is not the lack of time, it is the inability to achieve whatever is desired. In other words, if what you really want is, for example, to spend more time with your family, but 'there are not enough hours in the day', the real problem is not the lack of time, but that other things are robbing you of time which could be spent with your family.

Once this is established, it becomes clear that the true challenge is to focus on how to address what is taking up time now, and how the current allocations can be re-thought in order to achieve a resolution of the real problem.

It may be for instance, that two hours every day are taken up by commuting, or activities outside working hours may mean that by the time you are home the family is in bed. The task is therefore to think about those things that currently occupy your time and explore how you can either avoid certain activities, or how you can still keep them as part of your life yet carry them out in fewer hours.

For example, could you switch some or all of your activities to somewhere nearer to home to save travel time? Could you also, for example, re-assign evening events to the daytime, even if for shorter periods of time? Could some activities be delegated to others, who then reported key points back to you, so you still kept in touch, but did not have to spend as many hours in the office or travelling?

Could you involve the family in any of the activities that at the moment are keeping you away from them? Some executives take their children or partners with them on business trips or to evening events associated with work. Others aim to interest their families in their hobbies, so they can keep maintain their leisure pursuits and not lose time spent with family members.

Another alternative might be to try and involve your family in the business itself. Whatever the creative solution, it will be far easier to identify a way forward if you think about the problem in this lateral manner.

By dissecting the problem in this method, you should aim to identify two very important themes. First, what is it that appeals to you at the heart of your goal? Second, what are all the individual obstacles that you feel are in the way, and how can they be addressed to achieve your real goals?

For example, if we continue to work with our redefined aim, 'to spend more time with the family', we should first of all consider the appeal behind that desire. Let us presume that the appeal is really about spending time relaxing and simply being with the family: time spent talking, playing games, eating together, taking trips and generally sharing the day-to-day events of family life.

It can help to picture what this looks like. Take a few minutes to daydream and visualise the type of things you would like to be doing more of with the family. See yourself sitting around the table; picture all of you walking to the local sweet shop or to the baker for croissants on a lazy Saturday morning. All of this helps give a vividly clear picture of the goal and the successful outcomes you are striving for.

Once you have that clear vision in mind, then think about the obstacles. Write each one down, perhaps working your way through a typical day and allocating times against each item. Make sure the times are realistic not idealised. If you spend an hour and a half getting ready in the morning, then put that down, even if you are slightly shocked or embarrassed about some items. This act alone will often identify areas where changes can be made, where some modifications can release more time.

It may also identify other ways that activities could be varied. For example, you may see that in fact you are already spending a fair amount of time with your family, but note that you currently see that time as 'chore time': for example, time when you are busy cooking for them or ferrying them to events. One option might be to reappraise this time and try to treat it in a different light. Rather than seeing it as time for mindless work, why not try to make it more enjoyable and fulfilling.

This might be achieved by involving the family more in tasks such as cooking, or using car journeys to talk rather than listen to the radio or by avoiding reading the weekend papers on your own and instead spending time with the family. Rather than collapse in front of the

TV, why not sit with the family and watch whatever they are watching or even better, switch the TV off and do something else together? The point is that whatever solution works for you, what you will be doing is substituting an existing activity for a richer version.

Alternatively, you may spot items on your list that can be dropped, moved, reduced in frequency or held at different times of the day. One suggestion is always to aim to avoid evening work events, and instead arrange to meet the person during the day. And do not just limit yourself to lunch or breakfast meetings, which can often be time consuming and congested periods in most people's diaries. Why not think about meeting for morning coffee or in the afternoon. Meetings can be shorter, easier to arrange and just as effective, without eating into your time.

If you have to attend an evening business event, set yourself a clear deadline to leave after say 45 minutes. Chances are that you will have met everyone you need to in that time and you will have made an appearance. After this period, we are normally experiencing diminishing returns in terms of the value of staying at any event.

Another benefit of compiling such a time and task list is that you can assess which events provide you with minimum and maximum satisfaction. You can also consider which are essential to your business and which are not. It can be helpful to identify first of all those activities that are neither essential nor pleasurable; these are clearly the first that should be rationalised if possible.

The creative task prioritisation grid can be used to plot current activities in your current day and to assess their priorities. This exercise can help you to focus on the right issues and to understand what it is you really want. Otherwise there is the risk that when we look at things that appear to be the problem, we fail to see the real issue or to understand what it is we are ultimately looking for. If you can work out what the true goal is, then the creative solution will be far easier to locate; and equally important, the creative solution will have more chance of taking deep root in the way you work and operate.

It is only after defining your objectives, really understanding the obstacles and being vividly clear about the difference that success will make to your business, that you are really ready to find the creative key.

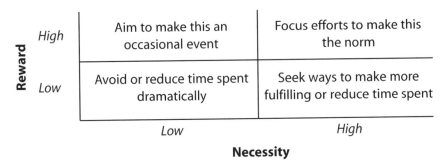

Reward	High	Aim to make this an occasional event	Focus efforts to make this the norm
	Low	Avoid or reduce time spent dramatically	Seek ways to make more fulfilling or reduce time spent
		Low	High
		Necessity	

Figure 3.1 Creative task prioritisation grid

Without this period of quiet reflection you risk at best coming up with ideas that will not work, and at worst, simply giving up in despair before you even begin.

It is only by understanding your deepest motivations you begin to open the door to creative solutions.

One-dimensional thinking

It is very important to have a least a basic understanding of how we think in order to harness the full power of creativity. Most psychologists agree that the mind works in two clear modes. We often talk about a rational side to the brain and a more creative, intuitive side. These two complementary dimensions work together to analyse problems from a variety of angles, looking at facts and information, but also calling into play judgement, emotion and a moral framework against which we make decisions and shape our opinions and values.

This book does not claim to be an authoritative text on how the mind works, but it does accept and take some well documented and understood ideas of how we all apply rational and emotional thought to everyday situations, and seeks to harness that process to improve creative decision making.

To make the most of creative techniques it is important to accept and understand that we typically have two ways of looking at a problem and applying our thoughts:

- *Convergent thoughts*: ideas which focus on solutions, facts, narrow interpretations and which are pragmatic and based in reality. Such thoughts are highly solution oriented.

- *Divergent thoughts*: an open-minded, exploratory, imaginative and questioning way of looking at things that is more playful and visionary. This way of looking at the world draws on imagination more and tends to think in terms of themes and big ideas, rather than detail of implementation.

Both these are valid and should be called into use with ease and confidence by the creative thinker in business. Unfortunately most of us tend to rely heavily on one or other of these ways of thinking. In business, there is often a strong emphasis upon the rational, convergent approach.

Discussions and ideas in the workplace are frequently judged in terms of numerical evaluation, with practical considerations being uppermost and at the core of many discussions. In business it is often only the route that leads to a bottom-line improvement that is ever considered. Clearly this is perfectly valid, but often many powerful ideas and sources of change are overlooked as a result of this dominant focus on convergent thinking.

When convergent thinking is the only mode used, there is no room or encouragement for the more revolutionary ideas that can come from divergent thinking. Divergent thinking is behind many new products that otherwise could not even have been imagined. Radical new ways of saving costs or improving services or of taking products to market are far more likely to stem from divergent thinking.

On the other hand, studies of innovative organisations clearly show that convergent thinking in such firms is also fostered and allowed to play an important part in the business. Successful innovators often also combine convergent processes with divergent checks and balances that ensure creative ideas are harnessed and delivered in a way that adds financial value to the organisation.

The obvious lesson is that organisations need to employ both divergent and convergent thinking in their planning and be equipped both to understand the difference and to employ the relevant tactics at the right time and in the appropriate combination. Only when both approaches are used will innovation truly flourish and lead to genuine business growth.

A negative atmosphere and environment

We have looked at a number of practical ways that we can school ourselves to approach problems differently and overcome obstacles that often exist only in our own minds. We now turn our attention to a blocker that relates to our external environment rather than what is happening between our ears.

One of the biggest blockers to creativity and creative problem solving is the workplace environment itself and the prevailing culture of any organisation. We have already looked at cultures of complacency and seen how they can tie creative thinking up in knots. But that is not the only atmosphere where conservatism and anti-innovative thinking can flourish. Firms that fail to make innovation a vital part of their existence are often doing so as the result of either neglect or deliberate sabotage of the creative spirit.

Creativity is a precious flower and will fade if the climate is aggressive towards it, or if the soil in which it is planted is lacking in essential nutrients. Negative colleagues and work cultures are poison to the living plant of creativity. And even positive attitudes to creativity, if they are misguided, can do great harm to this sensitive bloom.

A recent survey by the management consultancy PwC looked at innovation in business and showed that having creativity on the agenda was not sufficient to ensure that value was created.

High performers in the survey seemed able to convert their innovation into money-making schemes far more consistently than under-performing firms, who tended to find their innovations actually lost them money.

One of the most striking observations of the PwC study was the fact that poorly performing innovators tended to focus all their investment and effort into one big idea, while the more successful firms, would instead spread their bets over a far wider range of ideas and initiatives and throughout several departments and aspects of the business.

If you run a business you clearly need to foster a creative culture, but this is evidently more than simply supporting good ideas. The first step – and this too is borne out in the PwC study – is to create a corporate culture where ideas can flourish, be developed and be commercially exploited. This means demonstrating that new ideas are welcome, and creating processes and opportunities such as think tanks, working groups and brainstorm sessions, where ideas can be discussed, developed and harvested.

Alec Reed, Chairman of Reed Executive, the United Kingdom's leading recruitment and personnel development group, is also Professor of Innovation at London University's Royal Holloway College and founder of the independent charity, the Academy of Enterprise, which 'aims to unleash the nation's potential through the development of enterprise and creative skills'. In his own firm, Professor Reed instils a culture where creativity is not just encouraged but is extremely well rewarded. One employee received £100,000 for the idea of allowing anyone, even competitors, to advertise free of charge on the firm's web site, making it the country's leading employment portal and drawing thousands of visitors to see its almost 90,000 vacancies.

Employees must believe that their ideas are important and will be listened to. They must be encouraged and given the scope, the time and the resources to develop ideas into plans and bring them to market.

Clearly, this type of culture needs to be supported right from the top and reinforced through daily supportive behaviour and actions. However, leaders can implement other mechanisms, such as a designated board director responsible for creativity, dedicated creativity rooms for brainstorming sessions, or paid time out of the business for individuals to seek out fresh creative stimulus such as looking for ideas from competitors or in other businesses and leisure environments.

While such tactics are very useful in large companies – both for winkling out creative ideas and for creating a corporate folklore around the importance of innovation – they are tactics that can equally be applied to organisation of all sizes.

The people with the best ideas about how to grow your business are probably sitting out there in your organisations right now. They could be anywhere in the world, or anywhere in the office; they could be any age, from any background or perspective. But the chances are that there is a group of people out there that have some really refreshing and surprising ideas, and it is your job as a leader to maximise the likelihood that those ideas see daylight and are converted into money-making initiatives.

As well as the working groups, other schemes such as internal venture capital funds, creativity competitions, formal training in creativity, setting annual targets for creativity and building it into the incentive, appraisal and reward schemes can all help to institutionalise creativity and innovative thinking, making it more likely to burgeon.

Just as important as supporting acceptable behaviour towards creativity is being adamant about unacceptable behaviours that inhibit creative thinking. There is no room in an organisation for destructive, negative attitudes towards ideas for change. Business leaders must make it clear that a positive 'can do' stance is required and stamp on any growing shoots of cynicism or oppressive thinking.

Many people are naturally inclined to criticise and cast doubt over anything that is new or different. It is essential that this scepticism is not allowed to dominate and stifle free thinking and visionary approaches to your business. One of the most effective ways of defeating this attitude is never to allow yourself to exhibit it in front of others, since you as a leader will set the tone that others follow.

Another technique for turning negative observers and commentators around is to turn the tables on them. For example, if detractors are pontificating about how something will not work, or how they do not know how to solve something, try asking them what they would do if they did know what to do, or if they suddenly did have enough time, or resources or ideas or what ever it is they feel they are lacking. Though this may sound paradoxical, we have often found it breaks through the impasse and starts a flow of constructive ideas.

The individual will at least stop complaining, but quite often the outcome is even more positive. Frequently, the reluctant innovator will then trip out perfectly acceptable creative ideas and solutions, rather than the problems he or she has been so eloquently defining only minutes earlier.

Having recognised the factors that inhibit creativity in business, we are now in a better position to confront them. The next chapter will be the first step on our journey towards exorcising our fears and beginning to unlock the creativity that lies deep within every one of us.

CHAPTER 4

New ways of thinking to unlock breakthrough ideas

We have looked at some of the hurdles to creativity in the previous section. We examined both the constraints we place on ourselves and the off-putting behaviours and attitudes of others that limit our ability to see creative solutions to our problems, or even to see our problems clearly in the first place.

In this section of the book we will take a look at the techniques you can use to begin the creative process. This is the first step on the route to achieving creative solutions.

So what is the first thing you should do? Shut yourself in a room with flipchart and pen? Engage yourself in strenuous cognitive exercises? Well in fact the answer is – take a holiday.

Creative holidays and high days

What do we mean? How can taking a holiday help come up with good ideas? What we are in fact talking about is the need to take a break from the day-to-day to reflect and take a run-up at your problems with renewed vigour and a fresh line of attack.

This can involve literally taking a holiday. It can be wise to take a few days off and go somewhere different and new when contemplating a big decision. But remember that the holiday is a working holiday in the sense that you are there to gain time to reflect on things. All too often, our holidays today are as stressful as the rest of the year, with excessive sightseeing, endless socialising, over-eating, over-drinking and generally running our bodies at twice the speed they are supposed to operate at.

While this frenzy can be great fun, it is hardly conducive to contemplation of pressing issues. So if you want to take a holiday to have some fresh thoughts – all well and good; but make sure you go with that purpose in mind and be careful that you do not return from your break as clueless as before you went but twice as tired!

A creative holiday does not have to be a literal holiday away from home and work. But it should involve a mental and possibly physical break from the routine. You need to put in place a chance to slow down, to stop and to reflect if you want to make any creative headway.

We all need to slow down from time to time and take a look at things around us. If we crave creative release, we are compelled to change our perspective every once in a while to contemplate what is missing and what could be there to replace it.

The creative holiday can be something apparently trivial that you can build into your regular life. For example, it could be as simple as buying a magazine that you would not normally read, or doing something unexpected like going to a meeting of a group that you know nothing about. You might one afternoon go somewhere you would not normally go, watch an entire film in Chinese, use a pin to select a point on a map and try and walk there using as direct a route as possible.

You could try driving for two hours until you reach a pub or a bar and then go in and talk to the locals for an hour and see what happens. You could pretend you are a tourist in your home town and ask people for information about what to do. You could wake up one Saturday morning, drive to an airport, get on any plane and visit a foreign city for the day. Whatever you do or think of, these techniques are all about getting outside yourself and trying to see old things in new ways.

Sliding back to neutral

Whatever new way of thinking you try, it is essential to relax your mind so that you can adopt a stance of preparedness for creativity. We call this state of mind a 'neutral slide'. Imagine yourself as a car constantly working and moving forward, gears crashing, parts oscillating at high speed, energy being burnt up as you power on ahead; then picture what it is like to put your mind into neutral. To let you thoughts relax, to allow all the usually busy and whizzing cogs to disengage and slowly come to a stop.

Imagine yourself sliding to a mental standstill, your engine quietly ticking over, the steady rumble lulling you into a relaxed state.

This picture will help you understand the state of mind you will need to adopt before you can tackle your problems. It is all about going back to basics before you can start to find a new way forward. In our everyday lives we are often moving so fast that we do not notice or have sufficient time or energy to apply ourselves to our problems. When you want to go anywhere, before you select a gear you need to be in neutral and the same applies to any fresh thinking.

It is essential to stop before you can start.

This can be a natural process that the body will automatically apply. For example, in cases of extreme stress or shock, the body automatically goes into deep freeze mode as a protection measure. Fainting can release you from extreme stress or an adrenalin boost can bring about an enhanced sense of momentary calm in order to focus on the great exertion that is often needed to survive an imminent threat.

We believe strongly that when faced with business threats or challenges that require creative thinking, our first reaction should be to go for a 'neutral slide'. To slip into a peaceful state and then begin to think freshly and calmly before returning to the real world with a firm action plan.

This technique can be built into your everyday routine. It is a question of training yourself not to always have a knee-jerk reaction. To avoid the natural tendency to always search for a solution to a problem straight away, but instead to take a step back, to reflect and contemplate before acting.

While this may not come naturally, it is a habit that can be perfected and that can develop into part of your everyday thinking. The old adage about sleeping on a problem is brought to mind here, as a great deal can become clearer after a night's sleep and we can often take a more considered view the following day.

This is not to say that first reactions should be discounted. You should always listen to your gut reaction and when necessary act upon it.

It may well be that your first thought – even after extended contemplation from a neutral perspective – turns out to be the right solution.

It is the case that world-class chess players, for example, frequently think about moves for up to 30 minutes, but in the majority of cases they ultimately play the move they thought of in the first few minutes.

However, taking the time to slide into neutral on occasion, so as to consider issues, challenges and the state of your business, is a skill that should be learned as a fundamental basis for providing the clarity of vision and purpose that is at the root of all good creative ideas. If you can slow down and see where you want to go, the ideas will flow more freely.

What has tickling trout got to do with anything?

We have chosen the ancient art of trout tickling as a perfect metaphor for how we need to slow down to get the ultimate prize. For those unfamiliar with trout tickling, this is a technique for catching trout that involves no rod, line or net, but instead relies upon the patience, stealth and speed of the human body alone.

The technique requires the fisherman to prowl the river bank with great guile and caution, scanning the water for a fat lazy trout that is lying stationary in the sunlit shallows of the river, stream or lake. Once the prize is sighted, with great care and stealth, the fisherman must slow his movements down, reduce his noise still further and carefully approach the fish, gently submerge his hand in the water and reach for the cold-blooded beast's fat and contented belly.

Here – still being as gentle and calm as ever – the skilful fisherman begins to tickle the fish, relaxing it and lulling it into a sense of security that causes it to drop its guard and allows the hunter to continue stroking its underbelly while luring the fish closer into his grip. As the trout snuggles contentedly in the palm of the gentle angler, it abandons all thoughts of fleeing. At this precise moment, the hungry fisherman sees with a flash of clarity what he must do, and with lightning speed and determined aggression, he seizes the fish and whips it from the water, killing it on the bank and gaining a tasty meal.

Trout tickling is all about achieving a sense of calm focus, having stealthy thoughts, relaxing, being clear about your desired outcome, concentrating intently on your task – right down to the smallest detail – then choosing your time, striking when the moment feels right and turning that calm reflection into action that seizes the day and the glistening prize by using a change of pace to bring matters to an end.

Picture the trout-tickling fisherman and you will create for yourself a perfect role model for creative thinking in moments of darkness. In the techniques that are explained later on, you will be frequently reminded of the combination of techniques used by our fisherman on that sunny afternoon on the riverbank.

Using opposing forces: tight–wide thinking

Sliding into neutral to go forward is just one example of the paradoxes involved in creative thinking. Many people associate creative thinking with free thought, random association and unfettered contemplation of wide open spaces. However, our own experiences and the cumulative advice from creativity experts over the years show that this is not always the recipe for success.

Perhaps surprisingly, the best creativity often comes initially from disciplined and controlled thinking. It seems that you need to have discipline to be truly free. An analogy that demonstrates this paradox very vividly is the process of learning and playing a musical instrument. When you first begin to learn how to play, you focus on the basics, repeatedly learning scales and practicing in a very repetitive, mechanical way until the basics are mastered. Once chords can be formed, notes hit and sounds and tones achieved, the musician feels at ease in navigating the instrument, and only then can he or she move on to the more creative areas such as composing music, improvising and interpreting.

The same applies to creative thinking in the workplace. Without getting the basic structures and disciplines in place, it is not possible to make the beautiful sweet music of creativity. We need the framework of a creative process, to force ourselves through an artificial construct in order to arrive at surprising and refreshing solutions.

In the following sections we will look at some of those disciplines and see how they can be applied to free up the creative spirit and release the genie from the bottle. It will become clear that the techniques broadly correspond to the convergent and divergent modes of thinking discussed in Chapter 3:

- Evolutionary ideas and approaches: these tend to favour convergent thinking; tight channelling of thoughts to help refine and improve upon what is there already, or which build on a big idea by teasing out the creative detail that will underpin its success.

- Revolutionary techniques: these are more suited to divergent treatments that encourage more lateral thinking, take a fresh perspective and stimulate more abstract, visionary ways of looking at situations.

It is the ability to understand which techniques to apply and then to feel comfortable in moving from tight to wide modes of thought that produces the best ideas. Picking the right solution depends on the problem and in later sections it will become clear how to play this vital game of creative matchmaking.

Good pressure – bad pressure

As well as having the right tools in our hand, we often need the right sort of incentive or pressure to apply them. We often feel that pressure is a disabler of creativity, but the truth is that sometimes we need pressure to perform. Often short deadlines or limited resources or options bring out the best in us. Necessity is often the mother of innovation, but we sometimes need to apply the right type of pressure to induce the birth.

The trick is turning the valve by the right amount to deliver sufficient pressure at the right time. Too much tension can ruin events and we risk being overwhelmed and caving in, with creativity pushed aside. Too little stress and we end up as daydream believers, who are underachievers.

Stress has a bad press. But it should remembered that without tension the world could not operate. It is opposing tensions and pressures that keep objects from collapsing and falling over. The strings on a tennis racket combine to form a network of tension that causes the ball to fly at great speed: remove the tension and the shot is spoiled.

The strings on musical instruments, the reeds in wind instruments, the levers, wheels and cogs in an engine all rely on tension, opposing pressures and friction to perform. When opposing forces are well balanced and controlled the results can be startling.

The same applies to creative problem solving, and in the following sections we will highlight ways that the required tensions can be applied to the creative process in order to obtain maximum benefit without damaging the precise mechanism of your workforce and the organisation.

By engineering and controlling your environment you can stimulate thinking within yourself and your business. Techniques exist that allow you to manipulate all the variables: time, space, resources and so on. By learning to harness these tactics, you will feed and focus your creative efforts to great effect.

Visioning the future – dreaming with a purpose

We have already observed that one obstacle to creativity can be people's inability to look forward and imagine any other scenario than the one they are currently experiencing or that they have already seen with their own eyes. Earlier in this chapter we have looked at a few ideas for slipping into a more relaxed state of mind to help free up the imagination and dislodge any creative constipation.

However, freeing your mind to consider an alternative future or present is one thing; it is something else entirely to come up with a compelling vision of what that better future might look like, let alone plot a pathway along which one might get there.

This is where visioning techniques can be very useful. Visioning is just as it sounds: a simple mind journey that we can all take, whereby we imagine the future as we would like to see it and then work backwards from there, to see the path towards that nirvana.

It is a simple technique for learning how to dream with a purpose. It is a tool that can help us imagine different futures that are not based on divining the future by extrapolating from the present – which as we have already seen is limiting and often dangerously misleading.

The benefit of visioning is that it avoids simple daydreaming. It is a way of using the imagination but then drawing ourselves back to consider ideas and actions that will be needed to reach our ultimate goal.

There are several ways that one can approach this, but the following is a simple approach that we have found effective on many occasions. You will need about 15 to 20 minutes, during which time you should aim to have no interruptions. So switch off mobile phones, set your desk phone to divert with no ring, switch off the computer and close the door.

Get comfortable and relax. You may find some classical music in the background helps to slow your mind and free your thoughts. Close your eyes and take a few deep breaths.

Then think of the ultimate goal you are trying to achieve and paint as full a mental picture as possible around it. We have prepared the following example as a guide, but you can apply any objective, dream or hope to this approach.

Picture yourself going to an awards dinner for your particular industry. You are getting ready at home to go out; changing into your evening clothes and preparing yourself for a very significant evening, because tonight you will be receiving a lifetime award for services to your industry.

This is the highest award that can be made in your business. It represents a lifetime of accomplishment of leading your particular industry in terms of reputation, success and peer recognition. You are at the top of your game and this award recognises that fact.

While all the other awards are not known until the night, your award is a special category and you have been told in advance by the judging committee that you have been given the prize for a lifetime of service. Your acceptance speech is in your pocket and you know that in a few hours you will be up on the stage being applauded by your peers. It is likely that you will receive a standing ovation and a few close colleagues and friends will be cheering as you walk up to receive the award.

Try to imagine how you feel as you get ready for the evening's event. Look around your house: what is it like, what do you look like in the mirror, what sort of car have you got, what sort of furniture do you have? What sort of life do you have?

Next, imagine yourself going up to make your speech and accept your prize. How does it feel? What are some of the key things you know you have done that have earned you this accolade? What sort of things have people been saying to you when complimenting you on the award? What are the reasons given for the award in the speech made by the person handing you the trophy? Think of the memories it brings back: think of how far you have come and the things you needed to do to get to this stage tonight. Picture the working life you will have had to get to this point: the things you will have done, the decisions you will have made to achieve this peer recognition.

By now you should begin to have a sense of the sort of business you must have to be a success in the future. You should be clearer about the type of persona you will need to have developed, the habits you will have acquired, the attitude you will have to adopt, the actions you will take.

Once this vision is clear, think about where you will be in terms of your business and your life when you collect that award, and consider where you are now and the gap between the two visions. Try to see the gap as a shallow stream that you need to cross. What are the stepping stones that you need to put into the stream to get to the other side?

Imagine what those stepping stones are and what you need to do to secure them. Do not think of too many stones, just the main ones that need to be in place. Then begin to see the things you need to do to reach the far bank. Study every detail of yourself on award night and remember it. Think how you will get those things to become your reality. Picture yourself doing them and think about your plans to get there. Do not interrupt the visioning process to make notes, but use your mind to recap and be clear about what you see that you want, and what you see that you need to do from now on.

As soon as you have finished, take a pen and paper and write down an action list. Set deadlines for each action, even if they are years away. You should look at that piece of paper at least every six months. Diarise your review of your goal sheet and keep pushing yourself to meet deadlines. Be precise in your goals in terms of timing, but also in terms of the detail of your success. For example, use specific figures and percentages to track progress, rather than simply using general words or aspirations.

Visioning is a powerful tool that can be used over and over again. It can be completed by several people who then regroup to compare their visions and then go on to form composite visions of an entire group or leadership team.

Visioning provides the basis for excellent creative thought as it offers a vivid picture of the desired outcome and this channels the creative thinking far more precisely and powerfully. This simple technique can change your life. It can help you see beyond your current day-to-day constraints into a new and better world and it can provide the direction and spur for the radical creativity that will be needed to help you realise your dreams.

Lassoing those ideas

Soon we will introduce you to a plethora of creative techniques for generating ideas. But ideas in themselves are not the final goal. It is often observed that it is easy to have ideas, but far harder to turn those ideas into profitable enterprises. How many of us have had an idea about setting up a restaurant or opening a shop? Probably most of us at some time. But how many of us have actually done it? One in a thousand at most.

Creative ideas need to be brought down to earth eventually. They need to be tested and honed so that they can be applied. This requires a shift in the pace and nature of the creative process, a move from revolutionary thought to evolutionary development. From kite-flying to piloting with customers. The creative process is only partly to do with big-bang, eureka style breakthroughs. Creativity continues beyond that stage to refine the big idea, to make it a reality.

24/7 creativity is just around the corner

We hope that by now it will be increasingly clear that the popular idea of creativity being all about wild-eyed geniuses stumbling on world-shattering breakthroughs after fevered days and nights in the laboratory is only partially true. A far more realistic view of the creative process in business is of all people – not just the few 'creative types' – working in a disciplined and often quiet way on a wide range of problem areas.

Many ideas make for many solutions. A characteristic of successful organisations seems to be that they have a continuous culture of creative searching. They do not focus on the search for the one big idea that will change the world. High performance firms instead look at many ideas: some breakthrough, but also many that are focused on the smallest detail for opportunities to improve. They see gold in handfuls of dust. They cast a thousand flies on the water to increase the chance of catching a fish. They apply a range of tactics in recognition that there are many ways to skin the cat.

What is clear above all else is that, after a supportive environment and leadership, one of the most frequently seen factors for creativity success in business is abundance of ideas. Nils Bohr, a Nobel Prize winner, said: 'If you want one good idea – start with many'. All the research we have carried out for this book supports this assertion. Big improvements can come from big ideas, but for sustained success the right formula seems to be that the biggest improvements are made up of a million tiny improvements.

It is often better to improve 1000 things by 1 per cent than one thing by 1000 per cent. After reading the next sections of the book, you should find that you are able to keep up the creative pace of Nils Bohr. Before you know it, you will be having ideas all day long, and so will the people around you. The benefits will become apparent in every aspect of your business and personal life as you take more control of your own destiny through everyday creativity.

CHAPTER 5

The Creative Problem Solver (CPS model): Stages 1 and 2

Introduction

So far we have considered the nature of creativity, why we lose it, how we struggle to regain it, and the steps we can take to foster it once it is recovered. We have heard from effective, creative leaders from all walks of life about their attitudes to creativity and how they have harnessed this powerful tool.

We have looked at the importance of having the right mental state to really make the most of creative problem solving, and we have studied ways to be clearer about the goals and dreams we are aiming to fulfil through creative thinking.

We are now ready to take a look at creative thinking techniques that we can use every day of our working and personal lives. Over the next three chapters we will look at a step-by-step guide to better creative problem solving. Although we take three chapters to explain some fundamental techniques, these sections have been arranged in such a way that readers can dip in and out, selecting appropriate techniques according to the challenges they face.

The aim is for this section to be a regular companion in the office desk drawer that can be referred to as problems arise, in order to provide stimulation and suggestions as to the most effective approach.

We have grouped this section under an umbrella approach that we have called the Creative Problem Solver (CPS). The CPS model provides a simple way of thinking about creative problems. It has four stages, as shown in Figure 5.1.

If there were a single magical creativity bullet then we would tell you what it is. If there were a single creative problem solving method

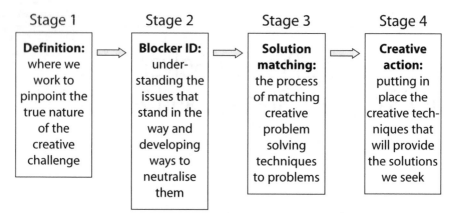

Figure 5.1 The four stages of the CPS model

that delivered results for every scenario in business, then everyone would know about it. However, the truth, borne out by years of creative problem solving work for companies across every possible industry sector, is that one size does not fit all problems.

The more we look at the role and importance of creativity in business, the more evident it becomes that there are many routes to solving creative problems, not just one. What determines the most suitable creative attack will depend upon the two key variables outlined below.

The nature of the problem to be solved

Different tasks require different creative solutions and later on we will explore some of the most common problems faced to see which solutions most frequently match up to which problems.

The extent of change required

If the problem requires a radical solution then, as we have seen, creative techniques that are divergent or revolutionary in their approach will be best suited to the brief. However, if the need is more a question of improving on an existing process or scenario, then the techniques summoned up should have more evolutionary and convergent characteristics. From running countless creative sessions, we have found this need to vary techniques according to the situation to be fundamental to success.

All too often, companies have adopted a creative 'way of doing things', that may well be perfectly effective in many cases. However, what typically happens is that this single process works well most of the time, but appears to fail – apparently inexplicable – on many other occasions. Unfortunately, no one approach will have universal success, yet companies continue to apply a standard method regardless of the situation, putting the variable results down to 'a bad creative group' or the fact that the ideas 'just did not flow'.

In addition, pursuing only a single creative approach is limiting. It can be too time-consuming on occasion, it can become stale and it always necessitates the same conditions – having a group of people involved, a room free and so – depending on the nature of the creative approach.

In our experience, not only do different problems need varying approaches, but on occasion a single problem may need to be solved through a sequence of creative approaches. For example, you may need to come up with the initial 'big idea' and a certain type of creative approach will suit this challenge. However, once the 'big idea' is confirmed, there may well be a secondary need to think about the details of delivering it. The challenge then shifts to coming up with several smaller bundles of tactics to achieve this. This could involve multiple company departments as well as cross-disciplinary groups working in parallel to delivering the same 'big idea'. This second phase will benefit from very different processes than the one used originally.

Variety is key to keeping your creative faculties sharp. And the more creative problem solving tools you have in your toolkit, the more chance you have of finding the one that leads to the breakthrough thinking you are seeking. In addition, having access to a range of tools gives you more flexibility to incorporate creativity into every nook and cranny of your business and daily routine.

Let us now look at how to select the right creative approach for the job in hand. The first stage in the CPS model is 'Definition', which is the essential foundation for determining creative solutions. Defining problems is as much an art as solving them, and in the following section we will examine in detail a technique we have developed, called the Problem Pin-Pointer, to help you refine this vital skill.

Creative Problem Solver Stage 1: Definition

'Truth hurts. Not the searching after, the running from.'

JOHN EYBERG

Defining the creative challenge: What's your problem?

If choosing the right creative problem solving approach depends on the nature of the problem, then it is critical to ensure the problem is correctly defined in the first place.

This sounds easy, but in truth many people find this a very difficult process and struggle to really understand and articulate what it is that is holding them back. People often misread the factors that are stopping them achieving their goals: they focus on what appears to be the problem rather than what they are actually looking to achieve, namely the goal behind the problem. This is akin to a doctor treating a patient's symptoms without looking for and identifying the disease that is causing them. Clearly, symptoms need to be understood, examined and dealt with, but they only represent the exposed ends of a thread, which need to be followed back through the maze to the root cause of the concern.

A good example of people's difficulty in expressing the true nature of their problems is the complaint frequently heard in the workplace, that someone is unable to get things done due to a shortage of time. It sounds reasonable, but on further consideration, it does not really make sense. There is no shortage of time: there is the same amount of hours in the day for all of us, the number of hours per day has been the same since history began. True, we are all trying to force more into our hours – sometimes voluntarily, sometime as a result of pressure from customers, peers or bosses – but the issue is not the number of hours in the day. That is a constant; the real issue lies elsewhere.

With further exploration, it will perhaps be revealed that the issue is really about the need of the individual to focus more on key tasks, or maybe to be clearer about those tasks that matter. Somehow, such people need to find a way to tackle fewer things in a better sequence, or to discard certain tasks, postpone them or delegate more.

Perhaps the real need will be to conquer their fear of delegation, or their concern over letting certain tasks be deferred. It could be their anxiety is that they will lose their job if they do not keep up the frantic pace, or they will be humiliated if they try to work differently and they fail.

Whatever the answer, the key is in really understanding what the need is, and often it will be seen that the true difficulty is very different to the original expression of the problem. We need to be adept at drilling down into our challenge to get beyond the symptoms, even past some of the real issues, to divine what the benefits being sought really are. Only then – once the desire and the benefit (the dream, if you will) is identified – can we really understand the true nature of the problem and what it would mean to solve it.

Not every problem is so deeply buried beneath layers of symptoms and perceptions. Some challenges are actually as straightforward as they seem. For example, a manufacturing director who wishes to reduce the amount of material wasted every time a part is moulded probably has a pretty clear-cut need. The wastage can be quantified and a reduction target can be set. The group then works on creative ideas to achieve this goal. The problem is well defined from the start and deeper interrogation is not required.

However, in our experience, many business problems are not as obvious as they appear on the surface. They invariably benefit from in-depth investigation, probing and scrutiny to really understand the full picture.

This is a key stage that should not be skipped, for when we have a better view of the challenge, our solutions are easier to search for and apply. To provide a framework to help executives really interrogate an issue the Problem Pin-Pointer acts as an effective non-confrontational process that you can use on your own or – ideally – in a group, to get to the heart of the matter.

The Problem Pin-Pointer

The Pin-Pointer could take five minutes to complete, or it could take an hour. It may be a brief chat, or evolve into a heated, strongly contested debate. Therein lies its effectiveness as a tool for flushing out the true nature of problems, for bringing to the surface issues that might otherwise have been obfuscated and for bringing into sharp relief the challenge faced by the business.

When working in groups, the first stage is to identify a person who is going to be responsible for solving this problem. It is vital that one person takes responsibility for the problem and that the rest of the group sees itself as existing to help this person resolve the problem.

This approach has a number of benefits. First, the problem owner should actually be the person who will, in his or her real job, be charged with solving the problem being examined. This ensures that the exercise is driven against a context of reality. If you are running a creative session where someone else will implement the outcomes, it is all too easy to develop ideas that look stunning but are utterly impractical in practice. If you are the one having to turn the ideas into a viable reality, then questioning their practicality is not a negative but a necessity.

Secondly, in addition to bringing a strong sense of pragmatism to the proceedings, having the problem owner lead the sessions, and everyone else effectively in a subservient role, avoids the familiar trap of the boss dominating creative sessions. Inevitably, he or she will set the tone and have a strong influence, hence the importance of encouraging and supportive behaviour as discussed earlier. However, using the day-to-day problem owner as the session leader will help to ameliorate this, as the boss in this scenario is no more or less important that anyone else in the session.

Once identified, the problem owner should begin to spell out the challenge for the group, using the Pin-Pointer. This can be done using a flip chart or a printed blank template on a sheet of A4 paper.

The pin-pointer is a simple flow chart that encourages the problem owner to drill down into a problem until its source is revealed. It also provides a framework for the problem solver to talk about the issues involved and the full picture surrounding any given problem.

The problem owner should fill in the first box in no more than ten words and then, with the help of group discussion, complete all the other boxes in the Problem Pin-Pointer as shown in Figure 5.2.

This process helps you to express the true nature of the challenge you are facing and precisely defines the exercise for you and your colleagues. When working though the Problem Pin-Pointer, you should try to be specific and clear in your use of language. As far as possible, develop goals that have a clear end point and a single

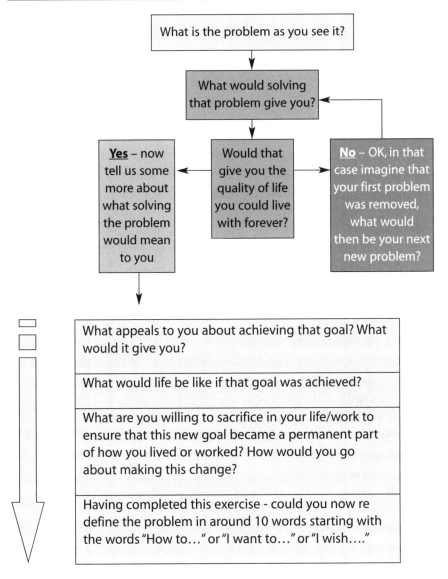

Figure 5.2 The Problem Pin-Pointer

desired outcome. If possible, include measurement devices such as timescales, percentage changes or specific measures of success.

A good example of a problem definition might be 'How to deliver our goods in half the time'. This problem is clearly articulated, it has a measurable target and it is tightly focused on addressing time-saving measures rather than other factors such as cost or general efficiency, which might confuse the team.

By contrast, a poor definition might be: 'How to be the leading firm in our industry'. This problem is very general and open to too much interpretation. What for example does 'leading' really mean? Why do you want to lead? In what way will it be seen that you are leading? How will you know when you have been successful? These are just a few of the questions that remain unclear in this problem. Its vagueness and the questions it poses clearly indicate that this definition needs to be interrogated further, to provide a more precise target for the creative problem solvers to aim at.

Micro-creativity

Even if there are many elements that need to be solved to secure the overall prize, it is worth breaking them down into mono-themed creative problems. Our experience shows that results are far more commonly generated, and more effective, when developed in response to narrow briefs.

For example, if becoming a leading firm involves improvements in areas such as product development, personnel, marketing, process development and so on, then have a creative session for each discipline that needs tackling rather than one creative session to cover the overall problem.

Micro-creativity is far more effective at pinpointing the right solutions than a scatter gun approach.

If we work through the Problem Pin-Pointer with a typical example, we can see the process in action. In this case, let us assume that the problem owner has been nominated – it is a department head – and has identified the problem as shown in Figure 5.3.

As can be seen, the original problem – how to find a high calibre of staff – is still there and remains an issue to be solved, but it has now become part of a solution rather than the problem itself. By the end of the Problem Pin-Pointer process, the problem has been re-defined as how to improve the quality of products. It has been agreed that this is the key to improved profitability, and attracting better staff and new sales are just part of reaching that goal. However, there

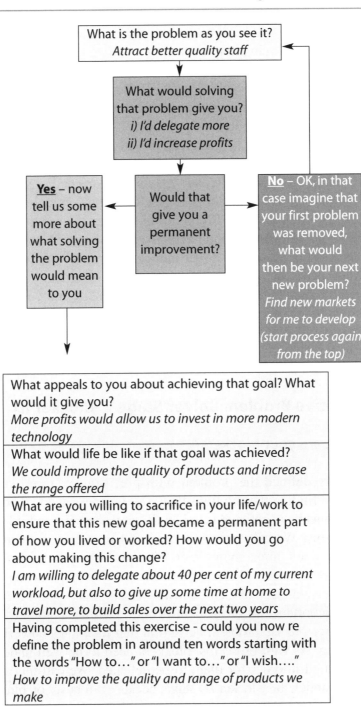

Figure 5.3 Problem identified by the Problem Pin-Pointer

could be – as we hope the creative process will reveal – alternative ways of improving manufacturing.

In addition to, or even instead of, more years on the road selling or the hiring of expensive new staff, there may be a whole range of initiatives the company could take to improve manufacturing. The benefit of the Problem Pin-Pointer is illuminated clearly by this example. Without it, the creative effort would have been focused entirely on hiring better staff.

While this is laudable, and may still be needed, it would have led to a set of ideas to support just one area: attracting new talent. Having completed the Problem Pin-Pointer, the group is now clearer as to the rationale behind having better employees, and they can also apply themselves to a larger number of fronts in order to tackle the main battle of improving manufacturing. The result is a fuller and clearer picture of the needs of the business, allowing for several creative initiatives to be employed to tackle all elements, not just the first one that comes to mind prior to further analysis by the Problem Pin-Pointer.

Creative Problem Solver Stage 2: Blocker ID

What are your blockers?

Having defined the problem with precision, you are well on your way to finding the solutions that your business needs. The next stage that must be negotiated is to identify any obstacles to finding creative solutions. We call these blockers, and they exist in many different forms, even threatening the creative problem solving process itself.

Later on, we will show you how to develop strategies to remove blockers, but first of all we must be clear about what the blockers are. The importance of clear identification follows a similar logic to the need for precise problem definition that facilitates powerful solution finding. As with problems, blockers need to be well understood and identified in order for them to be defeated. We call this stage of the CPS model, the Blocker ID stage, because it focuses on pinning blockers down, depicting them clearly and then making them vanish, or at the very least fade into the background.

From our research and experience of working in industry, we see that business blockers to creative ideas and commercial progress, typically fall into five main categories:

■ *Macro-blockers*. These act on a national or global scale over which most of us have little or no control, but generally apply to everyone (unlike fixed blockers, which only apply to the specific business in question). Macro-blockers include hurdles such as the state of the national and global economies, interest rates, legislation that controls an industry, trade agreements and rules, codes of conduct, regulations, levels of taxation and the cost of items such as business rates, utility charges, transport costs, postage and other infrastructure charges.

■ *Fixed blockers*. These are obstacles that are seen as being rooted in the facts of the immediate world around us. As factors that cannot easily be changed or are largely beyond our control, these reality blockers are the equivalent of 'fixed costs' in the creative problem solving accounts. Examples include numbers of working hours in the day, who we are, our age, our skills, experiences, geographic location, abilities, and resources – especially money.

■ *External blockers*. These are similar to internal blockers, but they emanate from other stakeholders of the business and from competitors. They might be the reluctance of customers to change, the aggression and scale of the competition, the limitations of the product or the market, the mature nature of the industry, international variations in product formats or standards, differing consumption patterns and tastes in different markets, the cost of expansion and restrictions on trade in general.

■ *Internal blockers*. These restrictions exist with any business, and are changeable – possibly in the long run – but remain fixed for now. These can typically include lack of resources, lack of scale, a shortage of budget for investments in new areas, fear of failure or an immediate lack of inspiration and ideas about what to do next.

■ *Fat blockers*. Finally we come to a set of blockers which are more akin to the seven deadly sins than to modern business problems. Despite the fact that it is very much within our own power to fight off fat blockers, they can sometimes be the most powerful hindrance to commercial progress. We are talking here about too much success, which can make a business complacent and stop it from seeking continuous improvement and dull the desire for innovation. Or complacency, a feature that we have already considered and which is at the heart of so many corporate demises. Other fat blockers include stagnation, inward-looking behaviour and a loss of a sense of reality. Laziness, procrastination, and being 'too busy' are all other examples of blockers of a more human nature, which can frequently be identified as reasons for not investing time and effort in innovation and exploring new creative solutions.

Not all blockers are created equal. Many are real and will require some lateral thought to either bypass them or accept and integrate them into business processes rather than being a continual source of concern.

Far more, however, are imaginary – or rather, they do exist, but they are certainly not fixed and they can be challenged or sidestepped. Upon further examination – which we shall do in a moment – many blockers are in fact truly irrelevant. Others are genuinely serious issues, but a solution is readily found after a short period of creative thought. The key thing to remember when contemplating your blockers is to view them all as removable and irrelevant. This is the attitude that truly successful business leaders take. They let nothing stand in their way and in the following sections we will show you how to develop a similarly courageous approach to blocker busting.

The blocker audit

Having worked on pinpointing your true problem, which is essential for creative success, we now need an effective and easy-to-follow process to identify blockers – real or imaginary – before we blow them up and see through to the creative solutions at the end of the tunnel. In this section we will examine how to detonate your blockers: how to blast them out of the way and move on.

We can see the importance of gaining clarity in this area, when we consider the debilitating effect blockers can have upon us. As with problems and goals, most people are not clear about what is really stopping them from getting what they want. They all too often confuse problems with their goals.

Take, for example, people who say: 'if I had more money I would be happy', They are really missing the point if they conclude that 'lack of money' is the blocker to happiness. They believe that getting more money is both the goal and the blocker to happiness. In these simple terms, their goal may be true, but in terms of developing a strategy to resolve the dilemma, it is a complete over-simplification of the situation.

They need to drill into the situation more deeply in order to really understand the drivers behind the true goal. After a short period of interrogation the true goal may well be revealed as the desire to be happy; further exploration might show that while more money might be part of the solution, it is not the only answer. This is a simple example, but it does serve to illustrate the ways in which many people fail to achieve sufficient insight and vision surrounding their true desired outcome.

This is bad enough, but often the problem is further compounded by apparent blockers that most people cannot imagine solving, or even tackling. Often we feel that there are things in our way that are just facts of life. People who are high achievers never see obstacles or life in this way. They ignore problems or simply think of ways of outwitting them. You can learn to do this too by learning how to really understand your blockers.

By asking some basic questions – are they really what are blocking you? do they really matter as much as you think? are they really there at all? what would happen if they vanished? – we can often dismiss obstacles and fears and liberate our creative minds.

Here we give readers a process similar to the Problem Pin-Pointer for use with obstacles. This methodology encourages you to really thing about blockers: to look them straight in the face and dare them to disappear!

The first step is to conduct a BAC analysis (blocker audit and critique) starting with your pin-pointed problem. Then list your top five blockers to the successful resolution of your pin-pointed problem.

Then take each blocker in turn and analyse it using the questions shown in Figure 5.4. At the end of the process you should have far greater clarity about what really is a problem and how to solve it, and which issues are really no more than mirages that, when faced, will vanish in the air.

The process of working your way through the BAC analysis should at the very least help you to assess and think through your blockers, ideally casting fresh light on them. It should also help you see how to remove them or how to ignore them.

Even if you work your way through the BAC analysis and the answer to the final question is 'yes', you should not despair. This discovery should prompt you to consider two new questions which other wise would have lain hidden:

1. Do you need to amend the original problem, or add one more to the list? (In other words, should the real problem be to first solve the blocker?)

2. What is the worst that would happen if you ignored the blocker? It is worth considering this scenario as it may be that the cost of ignoring the blocker is not as high as you might think and may be worthwhile, if the benefit is great enough. For example, one cost of ignoring a blocker might be a high level of waste or of packaging, but the extra packaging cost could be passed on in premium pricing and the waste could be re-cycled or a new market could be found for it.

In order to demonstrate the BAC analysis further, let us take the original problem identified by the Problem Pin-Pointer process and run it as an illustration of how the BAC analysis might work in practice.

You will remember that the redefined problem was 'How to improve the quality and range of products we make'. The BAC analysis is shown in Figure 5.5. As can be seen, practical steps have been identified to deal with each issue. They may not be immediately resolved, and even if they are, they may not be the final answer, but at least there is now a clear, easy-to-follow game plan for tackling the blockers.

Following on from the BAC analysis it can be worth developing an additional blocker-busting plan that sets out a clear strategy for

	Blocker 1	Blocker 2	Blocker 3	Blocker 4	Blocker 5
Pinpointed Problem 'I want to ....'					
General description					
What could you do if the blocker was removed?					
What benefit would that give you?					
What solution would you try if you knew you would be successful?					
What goal could you set to deal with this blocker?					
If you achieve this goal, will this blocker still stop you solving your problem?					

Figure 5.4 Blocker audit and critique

Pinpointed Problem: 'How to improve the quality and range of products we make'					
	Blocker 1	Blocker 2	Blocker 3	Blocker 4	Blocker 5
General description	Lack of funding	Outdated equipment	Unskilled workforce	Current customers not interested	Distribution channels not set up
What could you do if the blocker was removed?	Invest in new equipment and hire skilled staff, also invest in new distributors	Produce better product and more variety	Free up more time to develop the business	Increase sales to new type of market	Broaden outlets where product available
What benefit would that give you?	Our products would be better, the business would be more varied and interesting and our scale would be greater	A larger more influential firm that could take a leading position	Create more interesting and impressive business	More variety and interesting work, travel and range of contacts	Rapid expansion and new challenges
What solution would you try if you knew you would be successful?	Approach bank for a loan	Approach machinery manufacturer and discuss a lease and finance package	Headhunt from rivals	Hire telemarketing firm to identify new customer base	Franchise current distribution into new areas
What goal could you set to deal with this blocker?	Raise £5 million – find out what it would take to make this possible	Meet two leasing firms this month	Make four calls this week	Attend trade exhibition and arrange to meet four customers that have never been met before	Have one pilot franchise up and running within four months
If you achieve this goal, will this blocker still stop you solving your problem?	No	Possibly	Possibly	Possibly	Possibly

Figure 5.5 BAC analysis of quality improvement problem

success, including milestones to measure progress and give a sense of the desired timing.

Having run through the BAC analysis, you should feel more confident and better equipped to reach out for the creative solutions you need, without feeling distracted by obstacles. You will now have a clear sense of how to deal with these problems and be ready to move on to the next stage of the CPS model and start to shape creative solutions for your business challenges.

CHAPTER 6

The Creative Problem Solver: Stages 3 and 4

Having identified the right problem and despatched any obstacles, we now turn to what could be considered the meat of the CPS model: the matching of creative solutions to identified problems. We therefore now turn to the third stage in the CPS model, which is 'Solution Matching'.

Creative Problem Solver Stage 3: Solution Matching

Picking the right solution

As already stated, the right solution depends greatly on the task. As we have seen, problems tend to lend themselves to either evolutionary or revolutionary thinking, or to a mixture of the two. By and large, problems requiring radical solutions will be better served by creative approaches that are revolutionary, while problems requiring more precision engineering will be better served by evolutionary creative techniques.

Let us first of all think about the typical problems where creativity or brainstorming sessions are most often applied. In the grid below (Table 6.1) we have listed the problems most frequently encountered in our work and through research for this book. Next to those problems we have indicated whether this challenge will be best suited to a revolutionary or evolutionary approach. As you will see, in many cases, both techniques could be considered, either separately or together.

This grid will prove helpful when selecting which of the creative problem solving techniques listed later on will be most suitable. The techniques are labelled under the two headings of Evolutionary and

Revolutionary according to their style. Some techniques combine both approaches: perhaps starting by encouraging revolution and then ending with evolution from the enforced chaos.

Evolutionary creativity and revolutionary creativity

The difference between these two approaches is essentially defined by the outcome you are looking for.

■ *Evolutionary creative thinking* is to do with fine tuning and improving what is already reasonably high-quality. For example, a process that works well but can still be improved, or taking a strong basic idea that needs refining, or building a powerful overarching theme into a fully tailored campaign that needs to be adapted for specific markets, nationalities or audience groups.

■ *Revolutionary thinking* is all about throwing away the rule book. For example, when the European low-cost airlines looked at the existing market, they took a highly radical approach, abandoning many items that were formerly considered non negotiable: doing away with tickets, bypassing travel agents, not having booked seats, giving tickets away for free. Revolutionary creativity will help you replace the rule book with something even better, such as a different business model for delivering products and services, or even helping to create totally new markets or business sectors.

The common mistake is to focus on just one type of creative approach. For example, evolutionary creative thinking is often overlooked in business. The phrase 'thinking outside the box' often encourages people to be too extreme in their creative thinking, leading to initiatives that are not rooted in reality, are impractical, or that are never carried into effect.

This can have very damaging effects and tarnishes the image of creativity. It perpetuates the idea that creativity is all about huge eureka moments and flashes of insight. True, these have their place, but creativity is also about the minute adjustments to existing processes that accumulate to deliver real change and points of difference.

Evolutionary creativity is creativity for the real world: it is about doing those 1000 things 1 per cent better, rather than searching for the one big thing which will make things 1000 per cent better – a common error as already highlighted by the PwC research and our own studies.

Both types of creativity have their role and should be employed according to need. Also, different types of people tend to be better at one type of creative thinking than another. It is all a question of seeing the challenge clearly and applying the right creative resources.

Some of the techniques we list can be used on their own, others can be combined. The effect of combining evolutionary and revolutionary techniques can be likened to a squeezebox: drawing in air as it expands, and then forcing it out through narrow pipes to produce precise sounds. This 'squeezebox thinking' approach is worth bearing in mind during the creative process. Frequently we are encouraging others and ourselves first to open our minds to the oxygen of new thoughts, and then focus down to deliver the right notes for a perfect melody.

The list of problems below is not all-embracing, but will cover most eventualities. See which problem is closest to the one you face, and then look up the evolutionary or revolutionary techniques in the next section of the book, to see more detail on how to apply the various techniques. Some of the creative problem solving approaches take minutes to complete, others run for hours. The duration and format is shown for each technique. Experiment by selecting one or two approaches, adding more if further ideas are desired.

Study the grid below to assess the right approach, then look up the suggested creative techniques (see pp. 98–134) that are the antidotes to your problem.

Table 6.1 Creative Problem Solver Stage 3: Solution Matching		
Type of business problem	*Consider these* **evolutionary** *creative techniques*	*Consider these* **revolutionary** *creative techniques*
How to be very different	8,11,12,19,22,32	1,3,4,10,14,16,17,18,20, 21,25
How to be a bit different	2,11,12,13,19,30,32	3,4,5,14,16,17,18,28,29, 31,33,34
How to be the same (as a competitor, or someone else – i.e. a role model)	11,12,30	5,14,16
How to improve something existing	2,8,11,12,13	1,3,4,5,9,14,25,33,34
How to be faster	6,7,11,12,19,22,27	1,3,4,5,9,14,25
How to be even faster	6,7,11,12,19,27	1,3,4,5,9,14,16,17,18,25, 28,29
How to become fitter, healthier and mentally tougher	6,7,11,12,13,22,30,32	9,14,16,25,28,29,31
How to create more free time	6,7,22,32	1,16,17,18,31
How to let go and delegate	6,7,12,19,22,32	9,16,17,18,31
How to prioritise	6,7,13,15,19,22,30,32	9,16,17,18,25,28,29,31

Table 6.1 continued		
Type of business problem	Consider these **evolutionary** creative techniques	Consider these **revolutionary** creative techniques
How to have and develop a good reputation	**2,8,11,12,13,27**	**1,3,4,5,10,14,20,21,25, 33,34**
How to reverse a declining reputation	**2,8,11,12,30,32**	**1,3,4,5,10,14,16,20,21,25, 28,29,31,33,34**
How to hurt your competitor	**2,11,12,27,30**	**1,5,14,31,33,34,35**
How to destroy your competitor	**2,11,12,27,30**	**1,5,14,28,29,31,35**
How to come up with a good name	**11,12,13,26**	**1,3,4,5,10,14,25,28,29**
How to come up with a good slogan	**2,8,11,12,13,26**	**1,3,4,5,10,14,20,21,25,28, 29,33,34**
How to stand out/ differentiate	**2,8,11,12,13,15,27**	**1,3,4,5,10,14,20,21,25, 33,34**
How to change the status quo	**6,7,11,12,15,22,27**	**1,3,4,5,9,14,16,25,28,29, 33,34**
How to develop a new product	**11,12**	**1,3,4,5,6,25**

	Table 6.1 continued	
Type of business problem	Consider these *evolutionary* creative techniques	Consider these *revolutionary* creative techniques
How to create new variations on an existing product or service	11,12,26, 27,32	3,4,5,16,25
How to increase profits	6,7,12,19,22,30	1,17,18,31
How to do more interesting work	6,7,8,11,22,32	1,3,4,9,14,16,25,28,29
How to decide what to do first	6,7,8,15,19,22,30,32	3,4,9,16,17,18,28,29,31
How to make something look better	2,8,11,12,13,27	1,3,4,10,14,16,20,21,25, 33,34
How to get someone to like you	2,8,11,12,13,26, 27	1,3,4,10,14,16,20,21,25, 33,34
How to improve existing processes	6,7,11,12,22,27	1,16,25,33,34,35
How to improve quality	6,7,11,12,27	1,16,33,34

Table 6.1 continued		
Type of business problem	Consider these **evolutionary** creative techniques	Consider these **revolutionary** creative techniques
How to develop compelling messages/ arguments	**2,8,11,12,26**	**1,3,4,5,14,16,25,28,29, 33,34**
How to create a new area of business	**7,8,11,12,13,32**	**1,3,4,5,9,14,16,33,34**
How to decide what to do	**6,7,8,19,22,32**	**3,4,9,17,18,25,28,29**
How to have more of something	**6,7,8,12,22,30**	**1,5,16,17,18,31,33,34**
How to have less of something	**6,7,12,15,19,22,23, 24,30**	**1,5,18,31**
How to reduce waste	**6,7,12,19,30**	**1,18,31,33,34**
How to have better staff	**8,11,12,30**	**1,3,4,20,21,31,33,34**
How to have better suppliers	**8,12**	**1,3,4,20,21**
How to reduce mistakes	**6,7,12,19,30**	**1,17,18,25,31,33,34**

Creative Problem Solver Stage 4: Creative Action

Having matched your problem to a creative approach, all that remains is to select the chosen creative technique from the following list. This is the final stage in the Creative Problem Solver model: Creative Action.

Enjoy the variety of the Creative Action techniques. Use the problem grid to select the right techniques, or simply follow your instincts and apply to your challenge whatever approach catches your eye.

Experiment with the tools shown here. Adapt them to suit your business; for example, you may like to combine several together into a single session. Whatever your game plan, the chances are that the answer to your needs lies in one or more of the following techniques.

Creative technique number 1:	Creative style:	Time and format:
Theme catcher	Revolutionary	Facilitated workshop for approx. 8 people lasting 2–3 hours

Theme catcher is a structured workshop based on techniques created by the creativity firm, Synectics. It is a proven methodology, but it only works if the group sticks strictly to the rules laid out below.

There should be one person nominated as the 'problem owner'. This should be the person who is responsible in the outside world for solving this problem. The problem owner is in charge of the session and drives the creative process. The group also needs a scribe, plenty of flip chart sheets and something to stick them on the walls. The aim of the group is to provide the problem owner with actionable ideas.

Step 1. Defining the problem

The problem owner needs to define the problem/challenge in the form of a headline (like in a newspaper), starting with the words: 'How to ...' or 'I wish ...'. The problem owner might need to spend five minutes alone preparing for this. The scribe writes down the problem headline on the flipchart. Then the problem owner should spend five or ten minutes giving background information on the problem. For example: why is it a problem? What would it mean to you if the problem was solved? What is stopping a solution? What might be the answer?

While the problem owner is giving the background information, everyone else in the group should be employing a technique called *'in/out listening'*. This involves writing down any thoughts or questions that occur to them as the speaker is talking, but also writing down any absurd or random thoughts that come into their heads.

Step 2. Springboard thoughts

After the problem owner has finished speaking, members of the group should call out what they have written down during their 'in/out listening'. These are know as springboard thoughts since they act like a springboard in a swimming pool for a leap into new ways of thinking. Group members should express their springboard thoughts starting with the words:'I was thinking about how to ...' or 'I was thinking about how I wish ...'

Springboard thoughts should be based on each person's in/out listening notes. They may be relevant to work, or absurd, obscene, sad, funny, irrelevant or illegal. The scribe should write down all spring-board thoughts until everyone has finished.

Stage 3. Selection

After everyone is finished, the problem owner selects one springboard thought that seems really intriguing. The scribe then writes that chosen thought at the top of a new flip chart sheet. The group then considers this thought and comes up with ideas that might make it happen; again they can be realistic or completely crazy.

The ideas should be expressed starting with the words: 'What you do is ...'. The scribe should write up all ideas.

Stage 4. Actions

Once everyone has finished, the problem owner picks what seems to him or her the best idea, whether sensible or crazy. The problem owner should then be asked: Do you really want to do this in the real world?

- If Yes: Get the group to list pluses and concerns, then write up actions to turn the idea into reality.

- If No: Then the problem owner should talk about what seems most intriguing about the idea. The group then should come up with more thoughts that take the intrigue, but link it to a realistic action. As before, new ideas should be expressed starting with the words: 'What you do is ...'.

Typically a creative session will last between two and three hours. If you find you have finished sooner than this, you can ask the problem owner to re-visit the list of springboard thoughts and explore another one, repeating as necessary.

Creative technique number 2:	Creative style:	Time and format:
Story teller	Evolutionary	2–3 hour session involving around 6–10 people

Story teller is another structured workshop that involves taking a group through the following headings to create messages for specific audiences, target groups and sectors. The headings to be used in the session are as follows:

1. *Audience*: list the audiences that you want to talk to.

2. For each audience group list the *fact-based messages:* facts that you want this audience to know.

3. Against each fact-based message list three *proof points* that you could use to substantiate the message: facts and figures, track record and so on. If proof points do not exist, then list the actions needed to create them (e.g. commission research).

4. Repeat the exercise for each audience group, but this time focus on *emotionally based messages:* what you want each audience to feel and believe.

5. Then list ways that you can *reinforce* these emotionally based messages: how can you re-assure and build trust.

At the end of the session you will have the basis for a clear communications plan and the process itself will undoubtedly have brought a number of viewpoints to the surface. The debate alone is often very valuable in building consensus and a unified sense of purpose.

Creative technique number 3:	Creative style:	Time and format:
Kids' stuff	Revolutionary	30-minute power session, on your own or in a small group

Imagine you had to explain your business problem to a group of 10-year-olds: how would you do it? Write up on a flip chart how you would describe your products, what type of literature would you produce. How would you make your business appealing, what sort of events would you hold to promote your firm? Think about the type of people you could enlist to help you reach this group.

During the session you could try nominating one or two people to pretend to be ten years old. If they fail to understand anything or get bored they should let the group know. The group needs to work hard to portray what they are doing in such a way that a child would get it.

Then consider the problem you are reviewing from the point of view of a 10-year-old child. What sort of questions would he or she ask? What sort of information would appeal to them?

By thinking about your business and its problems from this perspective you will be forced to simplify issues and consider the fundamentals involved from the ground up. This can not only be refreshing, but can apply child-like naiveté to otherwise sticky problems.

Creative technique number 4:	Creative style:	Time and format:
Teenage kicks	Revolutionary	30-minute power session, on your own or in a small group

Imagine you had to promote your business to teenagers: how would you capture their imagination? How would you make your firm appear trendy and stylish? What techniques taken from teen culture might you use to bring your business to life?

Think how teenagers would respond if faced with your business problems. What sort of things would they try? What type of language would they use?

Try to see the world through their eyes and think what would impress them. Later you can see which aspects appeal to you and consider how they might be applied to your actual business problems.

Creative technique number 5:	Creative style:	Time and format:
Copycat	Revolutionary	Works well as a solitary mental exercise

Imagine something that you like or admire: how could you apply those attributes to your own business?

Think of a company, a celebrity, a politician, a public figure or an institution that you admire. Consider what aspects you like about them or it. How do they look, behave, conduct themselves? What sort of things do they say and do? How have they managed their career or history? What type of things have shaped such a favourable reputation in your mind?

List these attributes and behaviours and then think how you could apply these to your own business or specific problem. Maybe it is the style of certain type of advertising, the association with a celebrity, the style of packaging, the approach to business. Whatever appeals to you – explore the intrigue and the factors that impress. Think hard about how you could apply similarly impressive behaviours or styles to your own organisation or to yourself as a leader.

Creative technique number 6:	Creative style:	Time and format:
Oldest worker in town	Evolutionary	Works well as a solitary mental exercise or as a 30-minute power session in a small group of 4–6

Imagine you have another 100 years before retirement. Time is no longer a problem for you. Long-term thinking and long-term investment is the right approach. There is plenty of time to try new things: if they fail, then there is no pressure to catch up as so many years still lie ahead. You can take your time, because you still have plenty of it.

Imagine that this was true: how would you approach the business? What sort of hours would you work? How would your priorities change? What type of things would you still treat as a priority despite the longer time horizon?

How would it change your attitudes to work? To home? How would your day be different? Would you run the firm differently? If so, how?

By picturing this scenario, you will be seeing how things might be if time constraints were removed. This may well cast some light onto what really matters, your long-term goals (which perhaps have been neglected) and those things that really matter to you.

The truth is that although you do not have 100 years more to work, you still have a fair number of years ahead of you, and the possibility of change during that time may be greater at the end of this session than it was before.

Creative technique number 7:	Creative style:	Time and format:
Sleepless in battle	Evolutionary	30-minute power session in a small group of 4–6

Imagine you did not need to sleep and there were suddenly 48 hours in every day. What sort of things would you do with your extra time? What things would still be a nuisance and how might you deal with them now you had more time?

What would it be like being awake when everyone else was asleep? What would you do to fill the time?

This exercise artificially removes a common problem – lack of time – and therefore lets the group focus on what they are really looking to achieve if time was not an issue.

The discussion will bring out some key priorities and hopefully stimulate ideas for ensuring these are built into the real working day, as well as highlighting those elements that should be reduced or avoided.

Creative technique number 8:	Creative style:	Time and format:
Ovation	Evolutionary	Works well as a solitary mental exercise

Imagine you are receiving a standing ovation: what would you need to have done to have earned it?

This technique is all about envisioning success. Imagining the things you would need to have accomplished to deserve a standing ovation from your peers. The trick is to think about those achievements: imagine what you would need to do to accomplish them.

Then reflect on your current position and work out the gaps between where you are now and where you need to be, to be the receiver of an ovation. Try to see and list the steps you must take – along with how long you have to make them – in order to achieve the criteria for recognition.

This will help you focus on a set of objectives and be clear about what needs doing to secure them.

Creative technique number 9:	Creative style:	Time and format:
Outlaw	Revolutionary	Works well as a solitary mental exercise or as a 30-minute power session in a small group of 4–6

Imagine your profession was banned by law: how could you make a living? This exercise forces you to think about the things that really matter to you and how you would find ways to retrieve them if your life was suddenly overwhelmed by a major event such as this scenario. Outlawing of your profession would immediately destroy your reputation and cast you as an outlaw. To survive you would need to re-invent yourself. How would you go about it?

The challenge is also to think about what you would still want to do – despite the new law – and the ways in which you would go about it. Finally, spend the last half of the session thinking about the points highlighted and consider how these aspects can be applied to everyday business life.

Creative technique number 10:	Creative style:	Time and format:
Fame game	Revolutionary	Works well as a solitary mental exercise or as a 30-minute power session in a small group of 4–6

Imagine how a celebrity would handle your problem. The first task here is clearly to agree on a celebrity. It could be a sports star, an all-action hero, a political figure, an artist, a fictional or cartoon character.

Once the star is identified, the challenge is to imagine how they would handle the problem. Either spend the whole session thinking as one star or run several five-minute sessions using a whole range of stars with differing styles to vary your results.

As with all the sessions, end by thinking about and discussing some of your results. Is there anything your could take and apply to your business problem? How has this extreme viewpoint cast new light on your business? Hopefully the different way of thinking will have set free some innovation approaches.

Creative technique number 11:	Creative style:	Time and format:
Disney takeover	Evolutionary	Works well as a 30-minute power session in a small group of 4–6

Imagine the Disney Corporation took your business over tomorrow: what changes would they make? How would this highly successful firm tell the story of your operation? Would they rename products? How about job titles? How would they change the marketing? What would they do to the buildings? How would they go about dealing with customers and staff? How would they grow the business?

This exercise asks us to think about our business or our problem in the hands of one of the world's most successful corporations. We are empowered by this thought and imagine superhuman feats being achieved. This way we see what a dazzling success might look like. New light is cast over every aspect of our business as the Disney wizards work their magic.

Once this vision is conjured up, the group can reflect on how many of these changes could be made right now with the existing management team. Probably most important, by simply borrowing the Disney mindset for half an hour, you should be able to stretch your latent imagination powers.

Creative technique number 12:	Creative style:	Time and format:
Big Mac makeover	Evolutionary	Works well as a solitary mental exercise or as a 30-minute power session in a small group of 4–6

Imagine your business if McDonald's took over: what would it be like? This exercise is similar to the Disney technique and allows you to imagine the transformation that McDonald's would make to your business and how it might handle your problem.

Imagine for one moment the power of McDonald's experience in areas like marketing, new product development, international expansion, franchising and brand management – but applied to your business.

Think of the transformation. Think of things that appeal to you, but also consider the negatives. Then ask yourself what is stopping you from doing those positive things yourself. Reflect on the things you feel would be missed if McDonald's took over: is there anything you could do now to enhance those attributes? This is an excellent tool for allowing you to consider what ideas you could and should put in place to solve your problem in the style of Ronald McDonald.

Creative technique number 13:	Creative style:	Time and format:
Alien outpost	Evolutionary	Works well as a solitary mental exercise or as a 30-minute power session in a small group of 4–6

Imagine you opened a branch in outer space: how would you explain and set up your business for the alien market?

Spend the first half of the session literally describing how you would launch your business to an audience that had no prior knowledge of you, your products or even the entire market. Then link this thinking to your own problem or situation.

Some of these basic and fundamental approaches may trigger clearer, more compelling ways of marketing and communicating your existing proposition, developing fresh offers or entering new markets.

Creative technique number 14:	Creative style:	Time and format:
Chameleon	**Revolutionary**	**Works well as a solitary mental exercise or as a 30-minute power session in a small group of 4–6**

Imagine how your company would behave/look like/be like, if it was:

- a rock band
- a car
- an animal
- a TV show
- a breed of dog
- a country
- an actor
- a comedian.

Work through two or three of these scenarios in a session. Think about the things you would do in each case. Visualise your business or how your problem would be treated in every aspect.

Then pick some of the behaviours and attributes that appeal to you and think how you could bring that appeal to your own business or problem. For example, if you like the idea of large rock concerts, then you might consider holding highly staged and spectacular seminars for customers to talk about your latest offerings.

Creative technique number 15:	Creative style:	Time and format:
Second chance	Evolutionary	Works well as a solitary mental exercise or as a 30-minute power session in a small group of 4–6

Imagine it is 100 years ago. Start by writing down all the things that exist now that would not have been around 100 years ago. Picture your business back then: if it did not exist, what was the market like for your business? What was commerce like then? How was life lived? What attitudes prevailed?

Given all this, what would your business be like if it was trading at that time? Describe how it would have been. What was good, what was poor?

Then spend time thinking about how your particular problem would have been tackled 100 years ago.

Finally reflect on all these thoughts and consider if anything appeals that can be applied to today's business and today's problem.

Creative technique number 16:	Creative style:	Time and format:
Future perfect	**Revolutionary**	**Works well as a solitary mental exercise or as a 30-minute power session in a small group of 4–6**

Imagine it is 500 years into the future. Let your fantasies run wild. Picture how the world will be and the progress made in terms of technology and the pace of living. What will the world of work be like, in particular?

Given the powers that you imagine having in the future, think about how you would use them to solve the problem you are facing today. Then think whether in fact some of these solutions are not actually available right now.

Consider which elements of this vision are appealing, and aim to find ways to bring these ideas back from the future.

Creative technique number 17:	Creative style:	Time and format:
Starting over	**Revolutionary**	**Works well as a solitary mental exercise**

Imagine you were starting in this business again. What would you do differently and what would you still do the same. If you were facing your problem at the same time as starting again, would you approach it in any different ways?

This exercise allows you to mentally throw away all the baggage you have accumulated over the years and look at things afresh – and with the benefit of hindsight.

Finally consider what of this could be applied today; after all, tomorrow is another day. Who says you have to continue doing the same things as before? This exercise sets your mind free to explore alternative routes and pathways. It could be the start of some beautiful clear blue thinking.

Creative technique number 18:	Creative style:	Time and format:
Dire straits	Revolutionary	Works well as a solitary mental exercise or as a 30-minute power session in a small group of 4–6

Imagine you are in a poor nation. This exercise is excellent for forcing people to use their initiative and wits. The scenario obliges you to imagine you have no real resources, little infrastructure and limited access to the usual means of doing business. Telecommunications, IT, distribution networks and funding, for example, are all in short supply. Even travel is limited.

What would you do in such a situation? How would you tackle your problem? Imagine what poorer nations do: they apply for UN finding, they appeal to more wealthy communities for aid, they enlist the support of charities, they use the media to highlight their plight, they rely on people from developed countries to help them for free through organisations such as VSO. They improvise, recycle, adapt and treat every resource as a precious scarce commodity.

What can your business learn from this picture of how you would behave and think if you were in such a country? Think about parallel lessons and about ways you could poach some of these techniques for use in your own firm and to solve your own problem.

The purpose of this session is to force you to be resourceful, obliging the group to think of ways forward even though resources are limited.

Creative technique number 19:	Creative style:	Time and format:
First things first	Evolutionary	Works well as a solitary mental exercise or as a 30-minute power session in a small group of 4–6

Imagine your office/factory burned down: what would you do first? By answering this simple question you quickly identify those things that really matter.

Think about which things you would choose to do first to solve your problem. This will give you a very clear steer not just on what is important, but on how you can speedily establish key functions

As a result you may be able to speed things up in real life – including how you solve your specific problem.

Creative technique number 20:	Creative style:	Time and format:
Star struck	Revolutionary	Works well as a solitary mental exercise or as a 30-minute power session in a small group of 4–6

Imagine your favourite film star was coming to visit for the day. What would you do to impress him or her? Remember you are being visited by a person who is at the pinnacle of their profession. An individual who is used to living and seeing life at its most glamorous and luxurious and who is flattered and feted wherever they go. Also remember that this is someone you really admire and are very exited about meeting.

Picture how you would present your firm, how you would describe it, what the building would look like, what sort of food and drink you would serve, what sort of impression you would want to give, the gift you would present and so on.

Then translate this into how you present the business to other important audiences: customers, potential and existing staff, suppliers, the local community and any others who matter to you. How can you ensure they get the star treatment too?

Creative technique number 21:	Creative style:	Time and format:
Feature film	**Revolutionary**	**Works well as a solitary mental exercise or as a 30-minute power session in a small group of 4–6**

Imagine a short film about your business: what would you like it to be like? Who would be the stars? What would happen in the film?

Spend time as a group imagining the film: who would be in it, the music, the style, the credits, the plot and pace. Imagine a scene in the film that deals with the problem you are looking at. How do the stars tackle it? The solution can be as crazy as you like: maybe they just end up shooting everyone, or a giant tarantula eats the problem.

With the mental film now finished, think about the portrayal of your firm in this fantasy setting and the way the problem was dealt with. What appeals or intrigues you about the plot you directed? Could any of it be adapted and applied to the real firm and its real problems? Action!

Creative technique number 22:	Creative style:	Time and format:
Heaven and hell	Evolutionary	Works well as a solitary mental exercise

Imagine a reunion party in heaven in 100 years time with everyone from your life: what sort of conversations would you like to be having? Picture the discussions and hear yourself talking about achievements you have made.

Hear yourself recounting a tale about the problem you are now facing and listen to what you are saying about how you solved the issue. Imagine you found the answer, it worked well and you are now explaining what you did. You may want to try out several versions of the anecdote to see which ones sounds the most credible.

By freeing yourself up to think positively in this way, you may begin to see glimmers of light that indicate a way ahead. By imagining a noble future picture, we can often gain a better perspective on what we need to do and consider in order to make that future snapshot a reality.

Creative technique number 23:	Creative style:	Time and format:
Cashing in the chips	Evolutionary	Works well as a solitary mental exercise

If you are the owner:

Imagine you sold your business and you are now an employee. In this scenario you are rich to the extent that you need never work again. Work for you is a sort of hobby, you will only do those things that you enjoy and feel are worthwhile.

You no longer need to worry about the business in the same way as before. You have no vested interests; you are only keen to do what is best for the firm and for your personal career satisfaction.

What would you do? What sort of changes would you make to the business and to your life style? By forcing yourself to think about these things, you are pushing your mind to focus on the details that matter, and freeing your brain to consider the optimal strategic moves for the business, not those that serve other interests.

What does this teach you about your problem? Can you apply any of these insights here and now?

Creative technique number 24:	Creative style:	Time and format:
All yours!	**Revolutionary**	**Works well as a solitary mental exercise or with a close group of trusted colleagues**

If you are not the owner:

Imagine you bought 100 per cent of the business tomorrow. In this exercise, you suddenly find yourself in a position where the money being spent is yours and the money being made is also yours.

You take the risks and the benefits in full measure. How would it change the way you look at your problem? How does it change the way you see your role and your colleagues? And how does it influence your decision-making behaviour?

What does this tell you about your real life problem and how you might think about tackling it differently?

Creative technique number 25:	Creative style:	Time and format:
Magic powers	**Revolutionary**	**Works well as an hour-long session in a group of 6–10**

Imagine your brand, product or service had magic powers: what would these magic powers be and what would they do to the world? This is a brilliant exercise that is a lot of fun and can be highly instructive.

The group should imagine that your product or company has magic powers: for example your employees all have X-ray vision, or can fly. The important thing is to select magic powers that actually are related to your line of business. So for example if you are an insurance firm, it would be really useful to be able to see into the future as this would help you to price policy premiums. Or, if you make a product that helps production lines run faster with less energy, it would be fabulous if your product could be applied using a magic dust as you flew over your customers' factories.

Identify one magic power that is most closely associated with either your business or the product or service you provide.

Then imagine that magic being communicated in your advertising and being applied to your new product development programme. How close could you get to making that power really come true in what you do?

Also, if you really had this magic power, how would you use it to solve your specific problem?

Once this phase is complete – after about 30 or 40 minutes – you can think about what appeals to you in all this. How could you make something like these magic powers a reality in what you offer? How close could you get? Could you use this theme in your advertising or in the way you describe your products and services and the benefits?

Sometimes by using the language of magic and fairy tales, we are triggered to have heroic thoughts that can be applied to our everyday situations.

Creative technique number 26:	Creative style:	Time and format:
Wordsworthy	Evolutionary	Works well as a solitary mental exercise

Think of 14 words that you like, and use them in a 20-word description of your overall business goals. By selecting fun and inspirational words and forcing yourself to apply them to your business, you can often end up depicting your situation in a far more moving and engaging way than you would perhaps have done otherwise.

This technique also ensures you avoid jargon – assuming jargon is not part of your repertoire of favourite words!

Look at this hopefully more poetic and inspirational description of your business and think about any changes you need to make to live up to the claim. Also, think about your problem and imagine how such a firm would tackle the problem: it may be that from a more splendid viewpoint, the way ahead is more vividly depicted.

Creative technique number 27:	Creative style:	Time and format:
Getting better all the time	**Evolutionary and revolutionary**	**Works well as a solitary mental exercise or as a 30-minute power session in a small group of 4–6**

List three things you could do to offer a better service regardless of cost – then list another six, then another 12. This needs to be run as a high-energy session with the group or on your own, shooting out ideas to improve the service you provide.

The process of building up the numbers is a way of easing people into the exercise. Without doubt you will have list of 21 great ideas to make you even more competitive.

If any are prohibitively expensive, identify the intrigue in the idea and urge the group to think again about how that appeal can be delivered without the cost

If the ideas are slow moving, you could try getting the team to imagine they are different firms, for example: five minutes as Asda, five as Virgin, five as Harrods, five more as British Airways and so on.

Creative technique number 28:	Creative style:	Time and format:
Ideas or bust	Revolutionary	Works well as a 30-minute power session in a small group of 4–6

Think of something you could do that would put you out of business. Then take that idea and – for three minutes – write down everything that is positive about this idea. Then spend another three minutes on everything that is negative about the idea. Spend a final three minutes listing things that it would be interesting to see if the idea was carried out.

This technique is based on the PMI technique developed by the creativity guru, Edward de Bono. The acronym PMI stands for pluses, minuses and interesting. This simple yet effective technique obliges a group to consider both sides of a point of view. Even when the group or an individual disagrees with a point of view, it can open their mind to alternative thoughts. Once these thoughts enter the psyche, they can trigger new ideas under the 'interesting' section of the exercise.

The group may not agree with the original point of view or idea, but it is virtually guaranteed that this process of forced thinking will open up novel interpretations and modify a previously held posture.

Once one idea has been analysed in this way, the group can select another brainwave that would put them out of business and repeat the process. After three rounds of this, try switching to an idea that would be good for the business and repeat the methodology, asking the team to consider positives, negatives and interesting ideas, as before.

You may be surprised to find that the group is no more or less positive about the 'good' idea than they were about the 'bad' one. Either way, the end result is likely to be new associated thoughts and observations.

Creative technique number 29:	Creative style:	Time and format:
P45 time	**Revolutionary**	**Works well as a 30-minute power session in a small group of 4–6**

What ideas would get you fired? This is favourite game played by many executives. The idea is to imagine the craziest things you could do to get fired: everything from stealing or hitting the boss, right the way through to advertising all your company secrets on a high street poster.

This part of the session is tremendous fun and you will soon have a long list of hilarious ideas. Also think about your problem: what things could you do to solve it that would get you fired.

Then think whether in any of these mad ideas, there is anything useful; try flipping them and see if any insights drop out. For example, if you would get fired for telling your competitors all the company's secrets, what would happened if this was flipped around and you set up a monitoring service to track competitor intelligence more effectively? How would this help in your decision-making processes?

From madness, we often see a sane option that, without the excursion into fantasy, might never have been unlocked.

Creative technique number 30:	Creative style:	Time and format:
Turncoat	Evolutionary	Works well as a solitary mental exercise or as a 30-minute power session in a small group of 4–6

What would you do if you started to work for your most admired competitor?

This is another very powerful exercise that forces you to realise everything you know: your expertise, knowledge and skills. This power is brought home to you, by imagining moving your career to a competitor.

Think about what you would have to offer. The scenario also makes you see – possibly for the first time with such clarity – the weaknesses of your current firm. In this scenario, you would be aware of these shortcomings from the viewpoint of a competitor. In this situation, your goal is to exploit everything you know to damage your current corporation.

Also consider how – as a competitor – you would tackle the problem in question, not just to solve it, but also in such a way that your solution damaged your present employer.

From this point of view, you can see a vast number of new insights into your firm's weaknesses and its strengths. You will be able to take an unsentimental view of your business and as a result protect it from threats.

You will gain a renewed sense of your worth, and it will be a loud and clear wake-up call showing where you are exposed. This exercise almost always leads to powerful new insights.

Creative technique number 31:	Creative style:	Time and format:
Play clay	Revolutionary	Works well as 30-minute lunchtime session in a small group of 4–6

Make a sculpture of your problem using some modelling clay. Each member of the team should make a depiction of the problem they are facing. Participants then describe what they have created and what it represents.

From this discussion, some characteristics of the problem should be captured on a flip chart. The group then should make another model that symbolises a solution. Each person should then explain the thinking behind what they have fashioned from the clay for the second time.

From this discussion and play, many new ideas and observations can be unlocked. If not, the whole exercise is always most enjoyable and a great team building experience.

Creative technique number 32:	Creative style:	Time and format:
Cartoon capers	Evolutionary	Works well as lunchtime session in a small group of 4–6

Draw your problem now and then draw how you would like things to be. This is another creative play technique that asks the group to draw two pictures: the first of the status quo regarding the problem being faced, the second how they imagine things could be if the problem was solved.

Drawings can be detailed or abstract; quality is not important. What matters is pushing participants to use symbols to talk about their concerns as well as their ideas and hopes for a solution.

The use of symbolism is a well-tried method of communicating. It can be seen widely in literature, music and in all of the arts. Symbolism helps people to convey and understand complex messages and ideas. The discussion that surrounds these drawing sessions can be surprising and enlightening and will often bring up proposals for application, stemming from intriguing elements of the group's drawings.

Creative technique number 33:	Creative style:	Time and format:
Customerland	**Revolutionary**	**Works well as a solitary mental exercise or as a 30-minute power session in a small group of 4–6**

Describe what it is like being a customer of your business. We rarely put ourselves in our customers' shoes, and this task makes us do just that. By picturing the complete experience, we often see areas that could be improved.

Everything from what it is like to telephone your business, what the invoices look like, how meetings are run, what the product looks like in the home or the final factory – all these elements can make the group think about what it means to serve and how this aspect of the firm can be improved.

Creative business

Creative technique number 34:	Creative style:	Time and format:
A day in the life	Revolutionary	Works well as a solitary mental exercise or as a 30-minute power session in a small group of 4–6

Imagine a day in the life of one of your customers: think of everything they do, see and experience in 24 hours. What does that tell you? This technique encourages you to see your customers as people by imagining them during every hour of the day: at home, at the weekend, watching TV, out at restaurants, sitting in the theatre, playing sports and so on.

Imagining these scenarios provides an insight into some of the other environments and experiences your customer sees and is influenced by. This allows you to compare yourself with these other messages. Do you fare well or poorly? Are you an important part of their lives. If so how? If not, could you be more valued?

How, and when, and where, do you fit into their day? Could you be more convenient? More in tune with the rest of their day? More helpful in any way, even if unrelated to your specific business? For example, if your firm has city centre parking bays, could you offer these to your clients at the weekend or in the evening?

By seeing life through your customers' lenses, you will often realise a whole set of initiatives that can transform how you are perceived. You can also consider your problem through your customers' eyes. How would they see it? Would you be embarrassed if your customer knew about the issue? Why is that? How might you and your customer together deal with the problem? What would happen if you did a job swap for a day with your customer: what sort of changes would you both make and how might the problem be tackled then?

From this type of lateral thinking, novel approaches and answers often emerge, as long as the group continues to chase those themes that intrigue them and keep asking themselves how they can transform that appeal into everyday actions and initiatives.

Creative technique number 35:	Creative style:	Time and format:
Poacher turned Gamekeeper	Revolutionary	Works well as a 30-minute power session in a small group of 4–6

Imagine that you are about to leave your present company, which is in the retail business, to join one of your most valuable suppliers: the manufacturer of your most important product line. You will be joining the manufacturer as sales director and one of your first priorities will be to substantially grow sales to your old company, which is currently suffering from poor figures.

Now that you can view the marketplace from the manufacturer's perspective *and* enjoy an intimate knowledge of your old company, how will you go about achieving this goal? What key factors will you consider? Are you likely to be happy with their pricing policy, inventory levels and sales and marketing strategy? Are they focusing properly on the product line? By the same token, is the company you are now working for, the manufacturer, giving the right support in terms of pricing, lead times, product reliability, innovation, marketing and so on?

Would you be happy to continue dealing with your old company under the present terms or should these be reviewed, perhaps radically? Perhaps more distributors should be appointed in the region or, indeed, you might conclude that you are working with the wrong partner altogether and that alternative distribution arrangements should be made. With what you know about your old company's performance, you may even conclude that the manufacturer should bypass re-sellers and market directly to the end user.

This technique forces you to consider how well your sales and marketing strategy would stand up if fully exposed to one of your key suppliers. By trying to look at the problem of poor sales from your supplier's perspective, you will become clearer about what measures are required to resolve it. The technique also asks how well you *know* your supplier: their weaknesses as well as their strengths, needs, goals and ambitions.

Apart from highlighting inherent strengths and weaknesses in your business, this technique will help to provide a measure of how vulnerable your current business is to losing a key supplier, or being out-manoeuvred by a competitor trying to achieve better trading terms or – worse – replace you.

This selection of creative techniques should provide you with stimulating events and a great deal of fun. By careful practice of these methods through application to appropriate, well-defined problems, you should build up a valuable toolkit for everyday business problem solving.

In the next chapter we will offer some further advice on the practicalities of operating these creative techniques and of ensuring that the sessions run smoothly and effectively throughout your organisation.

CHAPTER 7

Making it happen: turning ideas into reality

In the previous chapters we have explored the Creative Problem Solver model: an easy-to-follow way of identifying problems, addressing issues and then selecting and applying creative problem solving techniques.

The CPS model is your key to resolving issues and inspiring you and your business to create those bigger and bolder initiatives that you need to keep one step ahead.

All that remains now is to consider the mechanics for delivering the creative solutions and embedding them into your business processes. The techniques themselves are very powerful, but if they are to achieve their full potential, they must be handled with care and delivered with conviction and confidence.

As a business leader, you will need to set the tone and personally drive these creative initiatives, fashioning the right conditions and support system for them to be used and relied upon by the organisation.

Let us now look in turn at some of the creativity infrastructure that needs to be in place if the CPS model is to be fully effective.

The physical creative space

Where you are when you have your ideas can be very important. While we will all have sudden brainwaves in all sorts of random places, we should also make the most of times and places where creative thought is most likely to blossom.

Let us first of all think about occasions when you are alone. Solitude has for hundreds of years been a state that has led to some of the world's most famous creative movements. Think of Wordsworth wandering lonely as a cloud, or of Gladstone mulling over matters of state while chopping down trees deep in the woods of his Scottish estate. These are some famous examples of where creation has come from recreation.

Many of us have enjoyable daydreams when we have rare moments to ourselves. So why not harness those occasions for creative thinking?

A number of the creative problem solving techniques listed earlier are suited to solitary contemplation. Alternatively you can use your own freestyle thoughts to drill down into problems and explore your true goals.

Try to think of those times when you are often alone, and typically you will see that you are habitually relaxed. This is particularly true when we are engaged in some physical or repetitive task or one that is a total contrast to our everyday lives. Good examples of where our solitude can be tapped into include:

- The car: long leisurely drives can relax the mind and free thoughts.

- The shower: there can be no doubt that the heat and the sound of falling water can help us to think.

- The garden: in the fresh air, tending plants or simply relaxing and enjoying the beauty of nature, our minds are often at peace yet receptive to ideas.

- The river bank: there is something about water that transfixes us and puts us into a reverie, which can inspire great thinking.

- The golf course: while the concentration on the game is intense, the experience of the open air, the walking, of manicured nature all around, can often cast a peaceful spell and stimulate calm, clear thoughts.

- The hairdressers: the warmth of the water, the enforced immobility, the drone and heat of the hairdryers and the massaging of the head all combine to make the hairdressers or barbers a deeply restful experience.

- Commuting: although dreaded, commuting is often conducted in a semi-trance. Our actions are automated, freeing the mind to drift and dream to the rhythmic sound of train, plane or automobile.

These are just some of the delicious occasions when we are alone, if not literally, then in our thoughts. Why not make these moments work for you?

Many great thinkers work on their own, meticulously picking over possibilities and options in their minds. Isaac Newton, for example, was once asked how he came up with his many brilliant theories; he answered that he thought about them a lot.

While solitary creative thinking is very valuable, it is not undemanding. It requires discipline and structure. However it is a technique that can be learned and after a while will become second nature. The trick is to deliberately make use of time spent alone and set yourself clear goals on how you will use those precious moments of mental solitude.

Plan your cerebral approach and intellectual tactics. Step into the shower and say to yourself: 'I will address this problem during this shower'. Or decide that by the time you get home, you will have developed five new ideas, or you will have made a decision on a troublesome puzzle at work.

There are many solitary exercises listed in the previous section that you can use to address your creative problems. Some last as long as it takes you to brush your teeth, others can be made to last for the duration of an afternoon's gardening or a round of golf. Many last a lifetime.

When thinking on your own, it is not so much the location that matters as the state of mind, which needs to be relaxed and peaceful but not comatose. This is why it is rare to have ideas while watching TV or a film, as the brain is set to standby, with the pictures filching the thinking and imaginative functions of your mind.

You can be anxious, bored, tired or stressed, and the creative thoughts will simply stay jammed in your head. However, you can be sitting on the foulest commuter train or ensnared in a traffic jam, but if you are relaxed, your creative mind will roam freely.

In contrast, when you are working on creative problem solving in a group, the physical location is far more important. It is your responsibility as a leader in your business to ensure that whatever space you use or make available for creative problem solving is as conducive as possible to the incubation of winning solutions.

It is worth considering holding creative sessions away from the office altogether.

However it is important to find a venue that guarantees confidentiality and a relaxed atmosphere where people can speak freely, as occasionally your discussion will be commercially sensitive. Equally important is a location where people feel relaxed about voicing ideas that may be radical or at first impression somewhat bizarre.

For this reason any venue should be fairly private and secluded; for example, avoid bars, railway carriages and restaurants.

The venue should help people feel they are a team and are able to be heard easily. Thus, for example, creative sessions in public areas tend not to be particularly successful due to the noise and distraction of such venues. A better alternative might be a long car journey as a team, or a meeting in someone's home, where the group will be relatively uninterrupted.

Booking a room at work can be just as effective and certainly more time efficient that going outside the premises. However, it is a good idea to make the room as stimulating as possible.

You could fill it with magazines from the consumer arena, trade publications, toys, Lego, wigs, theatrical props, incense, competitor leaflets, ads from admired companies, pieces of artwork, sports equipment, games. All these can be used to stimulate ideas and to get people jolted out of their normal modes of behaviour.

Often these props are not directly involved in the creativity sessions, but nevertheless people fiddle with them, play with them or grab an item to illustrate a point. On occasion, a particular object or illustration can trigger a further thought or be used to represent an idea. If nothing else, decorating the room in this way makes it clear that this meeting is a little different from the norm and that unexpected ideas and events are expected and encouraged.

You could try creating a room like this permanently in your firm and even calling it something like 'the think box' or 'the pressure cooker' – anything to create the right impression about the sort of work that happens there.

The London advertising agency, St Lukes – regarded as one of the most creative firms in the UK – uses its creativity rooms as part of its sales pitches to potential clients. St Lukes has several rooms in its offices that are totally decorated in materials taken from their key clients. For example, they work for Eurostar and have a room decorated exactly like a Eurostar carriage. Other rooms are styled to reflect the brands of various other high-profile accounts.

These 'brand rooms' are used for creative sessions and meetings, helping the teams to get into the spirit of the brands they work for. They are also working demonstrations of the agency's work and commitment. It undoubtedly impresses clients that the company goes so far as to actually redecorate its offices in the style of its customers. These brand rooms have become part of the industry's folklore and thus added to the creative appeal of the agency within the advertising and marketing communities.

If you do not have a spare room, how about setting up something new and different like a creativity caravan in the office car park, or a creativity tree house. This takes a leaf from the idea of sitting in one's garden shed and pondering the universe, and creates a separate place in which to think.

The absurdity of sitting in a caravan in your office car park alone should shake even the most stodgy minds into creative overdrive. Whatever you do, the objective is to create a physical space that helps generate ideas and stimulate free thought. At the same time, you are making a statement about how seriously you and your business take creativity. Setting up such a venue makes creative thinking a permanent part of the way you do business every day of the year.

As well as the room and its contents, you might also consider the provision of food and drink as part of changing the mood from day-to-day normality to something a little lighter and more fun. Breakfast treats, kids' sweets, cream cakes, beer, wine and nibbles can all help keep spirits up.

And finally, always try to have a sample of whatever you are considering in the room for people to see and try it, if at all possible. If you are brainstorming ideas for a new product launch, try to have the product and some competitor offerings available. Also try to source advertisements and other relevant stimulus material so the group can get a feeling for the subject matter for themselves.

Picking your creative team

Having sorted out your location, the next challenge is to select your team. A key part of making creative techniques work for you is to have the right group of people working on the problem.

This is not a question of pigeon-holing some people as 'having a good imagination' and others as 'not creative types'. It is more a question of ensuring that there is a correct balance between styles of people, levels of experience, background and character.

Some colleagues are best suited to revolutionary (expansive) thinking; others are more proficient at evolutionary (convergent) thinking. Typically, if you are looking for more radical revolutionary ideas, you would be well advised to avoid putting together a group of people with an in-depth knowledge of the subject. These people may be very creative, but they will be bringing a great deal of baggage in the form of personal experience and this can often be a hindrance when you are looking for fresh approaches.

When a room of experts is gathered – or even when one or two highly knowledgeable figures are part of a wider group – there is a strong temptation for these people to show off their expertise and knowledge of the subject matter. This can infect the group with a world weary 'we've tried that before and it won't work' mentality, which is not conducive to finding powerful new routes forward.

For expansive thinking, you should try and assemble people with varying backgrounds and experiences. For example, look for people who might have worked in different industries, set up a group with people of different ages or who come from a variety of backgrounds, races or social groups.

The fact that most of the creative techniques we recommend almost oblige everyone to participate means that everyone will – or should – have a voice in the room. It is often surprising to hear the views of someone who otherwise you would not consider to hold any creative thoughts when he or she holds forth on a problem at a creative problem solving group.

For evolutionary thinking it can often be better to have people who are technically expert in the subject. The group does not need to consist exclusively of experts. Try mixing in one non-expert for a fresh viewpoint, but make sure that person is not intimidated by the rest of the group. A body of employees that is knowledgeable about a subject can be highly effective when the brief is to refine the status quo rather than redefine it.

Running group sessions

There are a number of formal training courses available for those who wish to study the skill of facilitating creative meetings to a more detailed level. However there are a few key points to note that will help you get the most from any session you are running.

1. Create the right atmosphere. The session should be positive and focused on generating ideas. You must curb those who are negative or criticise others. Also, turn moaners around by keeping people focused on producing ideas. You might like to start with a ten-minute moan zone to let people get everything off their chest; but make it clear that after that only ideas and solutions will be accepted, not problems and complaints.

2. Draw in the full team. Make sure everyone speaks. Do not rely only on random calling out of ideas: go round the table, ask everyone to contribute. Set yourself the challenge of having each person speaking for about the same amount of time. This will mean curbing some and encouraging others.

3. Arrange for someone to help you stick up flip chart sheets. A simple point, but having to do them yourself can block the flow of ideas.

4. Try to bridge ideas and comments into useable practical ideas. In the closing stages of the session, try and get people to think about their ideas and how they can be applied to the business today.

5. Be disciplined with time. Never let a meeting overrun, regardless of how well it is going. Keep to the timetable. If you become known for letting meetings drift on, people will be frustrated and resent the time lost. Also, having a tight time frame helps focus ideas and maintains the pressure for quality not quantity.

6. Keep everyone positive, including yourself. Praise people for their ideas, avoid negative phrases such as 'yes, but . . .' or snap judgements like 'that wouldn't work' or 'the customer would hate that'. If you are not convinced about an idea, do not pour cold water on it. Instead try and draw it out, with a line such as 'I like that approach – what could we do to make it even more powerful', or 'that's a good thought – how could we develop it to solve our problem even faster or more thoroughly?'

7. Never let anyone say anything without ending up with an idea. If someone makes a statement or complains about something, do not let them get away with that being their only contribution. Ask them to tell the group what they could do about it. For example, you could use a line like: 'You are right, that is a real problem – what do you think would be the best way to handle it?' It may sound surprising, but often asking such a blunt question, causes the speaker to rattle off an answer that was spinning away in the back of their minds.

8. Surprise people. Another way to shake out creative thoughts that people did not know they had is to say: 'Just imagine you knew the answer to this problem – what would you do?' The replies that people often give to this simple 'trick question' frequently astonish the group and the individual concerned, who up until that point had been totally stumped by what he or she thought was an insoluble hurdle. Although this technique may sound paradoxical at first, its effect can be dramatic on a group that is creatively stuck. Initially in despair, people begin to speculate upon possible solutions or options: for example, if only they had more time, more budget, better resources and so on. Once these 'dream ideas' are expressed, the leader of the creativity session should encourage further speculation – for instance by asking 'how might that idea be turned into a reality?' Almost without realizing it, the group often finds that it has developed new practical ideas, or at least, is beginning to see a way forward towards a solution.

9. Avoid criticising or harsh joking about people's ideas. Good-hearted humour is fine as part of keeping the mood and your tone positive at all times. Never let your frustration show. If you think the ideas are poor or not flowing fast enough, keep

your exasperation to yourself. If the tension mounts in the room, the creativity will dry up like a puddle in the desert.

These are a few basic guidelines, most of which are common sense. Try to apply them to your leadership style in and outside the group sessions and you will be rewarded by people coming forward with ideas and thoughts that they know will be treated with enthusiasm and respect. The more your people believe that their concepts will be listened to, well received and valued, the more they are likely to be forthcoming.

Choosing your creativity weapons

Once you have identified the people for your team, you have a choice as to how they work. There are a number of options to consider. In some cases you may prefer to try a combination of methods to generate a rich crop of solutions.

Probably the most frequently used group formation, is around six or eight people representing a cross section of the business. The group meets specifically for that purpose and then is dissolved. This technique is highly effective and practical.

However there are a few alternatives, which we will now look at in turn.

1. Creative pairs

These can provide a very effective variation, with one or several pairs working simultaneously. This can be a stand-alone tactic, or the creative pair can be used as a supplement to the more traditional groups. Pairs of creative collaborators have a well-established track record in many walks of life. Think of the numerous successful writing pairs from the world of music, comedy and drama. Scriptwriters such as Galton and Simpson, Ben Elton and Richard Curtis; musical pairings including Lennon and McCartney, Simon and Garfunkel and Rodgers and Hammerstein are further examples of the power of two in building creative energy. The creative pair is an established feature in advertising agencies, with successful pairs often changing jobs together, for fear of losing the magic that their bond creates.

This phenomenon can be applied to any business, by selecting a pair of individuals who naturally get on well. They do not need to be from the same background; the key requirement is that they get on. They can be given a written or oral brief that outlines the problem to be solved. You can suggest to them the creative technique they should use, or let them choose their own method.

The pair is then asked to return in three or four days time with some fresh ideas, which they then present to you in person (do not rely on a written memo or e-mail alone). The pair are free to work on the ideas wherever and whenever they wish. It may help to give them a small budget for a few drinks and a meal, or to pay for some books or other materials to provide further input. You might also consider some sort of small thankyou gift, like a bottle of wine or dinner for two for each of the participants.

It is advisable to give an identical brief to two or three pairs to work on at the same time; that way you will increase your chances of success. The success of this technique will largely depend on the extent to which the pair hit it off. As this is difficult to predict, you may find that on occasion this approach fails to impress. However, it is our experience from across a wide range of industries, and from witnessing many creative pairs in action, that when this approach is successful the results are of an extremely high quality.

2. Working parties and task forces

The technique here is to form a semi-permanent group that will meet regularly – perhaps over a six-month period – to review and work on a creative theme on a regular basis. Groups can meet weekly, or every fortnight, but certainly no less frequently than once a month.

The task force should be charged with turning a big creative idea into a reality for the business. Such groups are effective at institutionalising any new idea into your everyday business and making it a permanent feature.

3. Networked groups

These are teams made up of people from different locations or divisions of the business who would not normally work together, but who have formed a group in order to implement and develop a particular new idea.

Such a group may be geographically spread, so meetings may need to be via conference call, and supplemented by e-mails. Some groups establish dedicated intranet sites for the project, to help share and store information and to promote an exchanges of views.

These groups – like the task forces – are very useful for turning ideas into realities, maintaining initial enthusiasm and for working through the detail needed to underpin and make real any new creative endeavour.

4. Mega groups

A final option is to mobilise huge groups such as an entire work-force, your customers, readers of a publication or an entire population of stakeholders. Mass creativity schemes involving large numbers can use techniques such as suggestion schemes, opinion polls, website voting, dedicated telephone lines and qualitative focus groups to gather creative ideas and opinions on future direction.

This approach covers two elements – on the one hand it is an idea-gathering process that seeks out a large number of ideas with the hope that the cumulative effect will be powerful, or that there may even be one or two real gems. The other factor is that it is a highly consultative approach, and such involvement in itself can be very positive for an organisation.

This last option raises questions about the practical realities of processing a large number of requests, as well as the need to find a way of responding without too much of an administrative burden, and demonstrating that comments have been heard while managing the inevitable disappointment when not every idea is implemented.

Nevertheless, well run, positively supported and recognised suggestion schemes are highly effective for many companies, saving thousands of pounds in costs and improving efficiency as well as providing a heightened sense of involvement for those participating.

Turning ideas into actions

At the end of a creative session it is often clear that a great deal of energy has been expended and that some great ideas have been expressed, but when you look at the outcome you see that you have nothing more than twenty or thirty flipchart sheets of wild notes, scribbles, drawings and diagrams.

How do you turn this myriad of crazy creative ideas into hard, money-making actions?

The answer lies in identifying the appeal in an idea, no matter how wild, and then building a bridge to transport that appeal into your business. This is a process that you may be able to apply in the creative problem solving session itself, or you may have to sit down with flip chart sheets later on and try and bend the raw creativity into fully fashioned business tools – either on your own, or with one or two other team members.

Alternatively, you might call another creative session, but this time ask it to focus specifically on turning one of the earlier great ideas into an action plan, perhaps employing one of the more evolutionary creative techniques highlighted earlier.

At first sight, an idea may appeal but on the surface seem irrelevant. The trick is to understand what it is about the idea that appeals to you and think what that could mean for your situation. Ask yourself what you learnt from an idea or a session that might be advantageous to your everyday business. Often the jarring effect of a wildcard idea will set in train another thought that may be the pragmatic solution to an everyday issue.

Not every idea that was good at its creation will mature into a winner. This is just a fact that you must accept. If you think of a good idea as a wild tiger – mighty and impressive but out of your control – then try and picture the appeal of the idea as being the tiger's tail. Hold on to the tail – the appeal – and try to follow what is drawing you on. Hopefully the tail will drag you to a fresh idea and a new position from which you can see your problem from a different perspective. Then you can let the tiger tail go and focus on the additional idea you have just unearthed.

For example, if you have applied the creative techniques mentioned earlier around imagining your business as a rock band (creative technique number 14, entitled 'Chameleon'), you might like the idea of album covers, roadies and groupies but be unable to imagine how this relates to real life. Well, thinking about groupies could translate as a loyalty club for your customers; the concept of roadies could lead to a network of special suppliers with whom you work in close partnership; album cover design might trigger ideas for more creative brochures; the idea of rock stars might lead to a program to build your profile in your industry; and so on.

Looking for these connections in order to harvest ideas into practical improvements is an art, but one that can be acquired with relatively little practice. What matters most is a positive outlook and an enthusiasm to delve into your convictions in order to find a link that could awaken a new thought.

This open-mindedness is the key to seeing how initial glimmerings in the mind can become valuable competitive advantages and strategies for real and lasting change in your organisation.

Evaluating creative initiatives: keeping the flame alive

There are several ways that you can measure the level of creativity in your business: you can track numbers of patents, assess the quality of creative sessions held, count the number of new products developed, or include creativity in your customer satisfaction evaluation process.

A vital part of building a creative culture is not only the tracking and measurement of creativity but also promoting progress in this area to employees and to external audiences. Promoting the fact that creativity is being measured and is considered important will position you as an innovative firm. Publicity around the number of creative ideas developed and the scale and nature of suggestions made by employees will add to the feeling that your workplace is one where creativity is noticed and recognised.

Make the time to evaluate creative initiatives and communicate the difference that they make to the business in extra sales, industry awards, customer compliments and growing market share.

By rewarding and praising creativity, you are more likely to encourage greater enthusiasm and acceptance of creative problem solving as part of the DNA of your business.

Conclusion

Having now worked through the CPS model and seen the options for its application, you have all you need to introduce more creativity into your business. The techniques described here are simple, practical and can be applied with ease and often at a modest cost.

Start small. Experiment with a few sessions; try working on your own, then in groups, before moving on to creative pairs. The more you practice these techniques, the more familiar you and your colleagues will become with this approach. All that remains now is for you to take the decision to seize the initiative and start using creativity to improve your world.

Index